# iPhone Xs & Xs Max
## User Manual

*Complete Guide for a Beginner & a Senior on the Latest Tips & Tricks of Using iPhone Xs & Xs Max, & Upgrading iOS 12 to Current iOS Version*

## Ephong Globright

1

# Copyright © 2020

# Facts Acclamation

This iPhone XS User Manual is primarily designed to provide complete solutions to several operational challenges on the use of many basic apps, technical setup, ensuring comfortability, and safe usage of the iPhone by the dummies, beginners, and seniors.

# Table of Contents

Introduction ................................................................. 9

    The In and Out of iPhone XS & iPhone XS Max Body Parts. 9

    Correct Method of Putting SIM Card into Your iPhone ....... 18

Guide One ................................................................ 21

    Why You Need to Upgrade iOS & Important Applications (Apps) ................................................................. 21

        What is the importance of Upgraded iOS? ................ 21

        The Importance of Applications (Apps) ................... 22

        How You Could Upgrade iOS 12 on Your iPhone XS to Latest iOS 13 Version ........................................... 29

Guide Two ................................................................ 33

    How You Can Make Your iPhone XS/XS Max To Start Working After Manual Setup ................................... 33

        What To Do First ................................................ 33

        How You Can Transfer Data or Documents from Old iPhone to iPhone XS or XS Max Automatically .............................. 39

        How To Place Old iPhone and New iPhone ......... 42

        How You Can Back-up Everything on Your Old iPhone Before Automatic Transfer ................................... 43

        How Android User Could Transfer Data and Vital Documents into iPhone XS or XS Max ................................... 47

Guide Three ............................................................. 53

    How You Can Use Default & Customized Controls On iPhone XS & XS Max ................................................................. 53

        How You Can Add More of Apps' Controls in Control Center ................................................................. 56

        How You Could Create & Check Your Customized Controls from Control Center ........................................... 57

How You Can Activate iPhone Screen Brightness from The Source ..................................................................58

How Video and Music Can Be Taken from Other iPhones to Your iPhone XS & XS Max ...............................................58

How You Can Use iTunes App on Your iPhone XS & XS Max ..................................................................................59

Syncing your iPhone with iTunes to Get Additional Benefits ..................................................................................59

How You Send Audio Sound to AirPlay Speaker from Your iPhone XS & XS Max ..........................................................61

Why You Need App Store on Your iPhone XS & XS Max ..61

How You Can Easily Fix Malfunction or Freezing Problem on Your iPhone..................................................................62

How You Can Fully Set Notification on Your iPhone XS or XS Max........................................................................62

How to Safe the Use of Cellular Data on Your iPhone XS & XS Max........................................................................63

How You Can Rescue Yourself with Emergency Free Call on Your iPhone XS & XS Max ...............................................63

Guide Four..................................................................65

How You Can Use All the Important Basic Futures on Your iPhone..................................................................65

How To Salience Ringtone, Vibration, or Notification Alert65

Wake & Sleep Actions ..........................................67

How You Could Rearrange App's Icons on the Homescreen ..................................................................................68

How You Can Make A File To Keep Two or More Apps On Homescreen ..................................................................68

How You Can Delete Apps on the Homescreen ..................70

How You Could Change Wallpaper of Both Lock Screen & Home Screen ..........................................................70

4

Homescreen Precautions ........................................ 72

How You Can Ensure Low Power Mode Battery Manager .. 74

How You Can Improve Battery Life-Time Through Auto-Lock Control ....................................................... 75

Guide Five ........................................................... 77

How You Can Create Security IDs on Your iPhone XS & XS Max ........................................................... 77

How to Get a Secure Apple ID on Your iPhone .................. 77

How You Can Correctly Do Your Face ID ........................ 82

How to Create an Unbreakable & Safe Passcode ............... 83

Activation of Apps in iCloud Account ............................ 85

Guide Six ............................................................ 87

All Apps You Could Use to Relate with Others on Your iPhone ............................................................. 87

How You Could Fully Enjoy Different Calls with Phone App on Your iPhone ..................................................... 88

All You Can Do When You Are on a Call .......................... 95

How to Set Special Sound & Hepatic Rings for Calls, Messages, Alert, & Mail Notifications .............................. 99

Guide Seven ........................................................ 101

How You Can Fully Enjoy FaceTime App on Your iPhone XS or XS Max ......................................................... 101

Other Ways of Using Message App on Your iPhone .......... 104

How to Make Your Customized Animoji or Memoji on Your iPhone ............................................................. 107

How to Fully Use Mail App to Get Good Results .............. 109

All You Can Ask Siri To Do For You Through Voice Dictation ........................................................... 116

How You Can Effectively Make Siri To Serve You .......... 117

5

How You Can Perfectly Use Safari App ........................... 118

Guide Eight ................................................................... 126

Best Ways of Using Camera and Photo Apps on Your iPhone XS and XS Max ............................................................. 126

The importance of Telephoto Camera ............................. 127

How You Can Control Exposure of Your Image ............... 130

To Restore AE/AF of Your Camera ................................ 131

How to Use Filter Options for Saved Photos ................... 131

How to Use Timer to Take Pictures ............................... 132

How to Record Video or Slo-Mo at the Highest Efficiency 134

How You Could Use Pano Mode (Panorama) ................... 137

How to Use Your iPhone Camera to Scan Quick Response (QR) Code ................................................................. 138

How to Use High Dynamic Range (HDR) Camera to Produce Outstanding Photo Shoots ......................................... 139

How You Can Use Professional Camera App To Boost Your Photograph Quality ................................................... 142

Guide Nine ................................................................... 153

How To Get Your Lost iPhone Back ............................... 153

What To Do After You Have Lost Your iPhone ................ 154

How You Can Use Another iPhone to Track Your Lost iPhone ...................................................................... 158

How You Can Share Your Location with Others .............. 159

How You Can Setup CarPlay Connection on Your iPhone & Car Stereo ................................................................. 160

How Siri Can Provide Solutions to CarPlay Problems ....... 163

Guide Ten ..................................................................... 167

How You Can Accurately Track Your Health on Your iPhone XS or XS Max ............................................................ 167

What To Do First................................................. 168

How You Can Set Up Your Health Profile ......................... 168

How You Can Set Up Medical ID ................................... 169

How You Can Setup Your Health Data ............................. 171

How You Can Check Your Health Data ............................. 173

How You Can Track All Your Favorite Categories with Your
iPhone............................................................. 173

How Organ Donation Could Be Setup on Your iPhone...... 174

How You Can Fix Failure of  Health Tracking on Your
iPhone XS or XS Max ....................................... 175

How You Can Make Family Sharing Working.................. 175

How You Can Use Health App To Track Your Menstrual
Cycle on Your iPhone ....................................... 177

How You Can Set Up Prediction for Period, fertility, and
Notification, through Cycle Tracking ................................ 181

Easy Ways of Knowing the Data Source from Several
Sources ...................................................... 183

Bonus Guide.................................................. 186

The Protective Accessory for iPhone XS or XS Max ......... 186

Reference.................................................... 190

Index........................................................ 191

**IPhone XS Max**

**IPhone XS**

# INTRODUCTION

iPhone XS and XS Max User Manual are an informative self-explanatory, and easy to understand guide that contains simple step by step tips and tricks on different ways of solving various problems with clear photographs and screenshots that provide a clear explanation on how you can work things out yourself successfully without looking for an expert to help you out.

For every individual that wants to know the in-and-out of how to use the iPhone XS and XS Max will really find this amazing manual helpful. This inevitable is easy to understand 2 in 1 manual for both beginners and seniors makes the use of iPhone XS and XS Max very easy by providing total solutions to many problems that include setup; upgrade; transfer of data or document from other devices like Android Phone, Mac, PC, etc. to your iPhone; application of latest apps; creating of customized controls, performing important settings for all essential features... and many others.

It is the best option for dummies and first-timers to choose for them to know the most essential tools of operation that can help them to efficiently enjoy their newly purchased iPhone XS or iPhone XS Max to the fullest. This book fully breakdown the technical terms into general understandable English term to improve the manual users' understanding of happily using their iPhone XS or XS Max.

For instance, if you are to enable any app's feature in the settings, the page(s) name that you will need to search for what you are looking for will be mentioned and what you are looking for will also be mentioned. You will soon read the details under the introduction.

## *The In and Out of iPhone XS & iPhone XS Max Body Parts*

On September 12, 2018, iPhone XS, XS Max, and XR were released together by Apple Company. iPhone XS has the same operational features as iPhone XS Max; but the weight, battery capacity, and the size of the iPhone XS are slightly different from iPhone XS Max.

iPhone XS is smaller in size to the size of iPhone XS Max and the Battery of the iPhone XS Max is one hour stronger than the battery of the iPhone XS; but every other thing about their speed, resistance, quality, technical efficiency, and operational techniques are the same.

| iPhone XS | iPhone XS Max |
|---|---|
| 12MP Wide Rear Camera<br>Flash<br>12MP Telephoto Rear Camera<br>Notch<br>5.8 Inches (147.32mm) — 5.65 Inches (143.6mm)<br>2.75 Inches (70.9mm) | 12MP Wide Rear Camera<br>Flash<br>12MP Telephoto Rear Camera<br>Notch<br>6.5 Inches (165.10mm) — 6.20 Inches (157.5mm)<br>3.05 Inches (77.4mm) |
| Weight: 6.24 ounces (177 grams) | Weight: 7.34 ounces (208 grams) |
| Height: 5.65 Inches (143.6mm) | Height: 6.20 Inches (157.5mm) |
| Width/Breadth: 2.75 Inches (70.9mm) | Width/Breadth: 3.05 Inches (77.4mm) |
| Super Retina HD Display Screen Diameter:<br>5.8 Inches (147.32mm) | Super Retina HD Display Screen Diameter:<br>6.5 Inches (165.10mm) |
| Battery Time Length:<br>30 minutes Stronger<br>than iPhone X | Battery Time Length:<br>2 Hours Stronger<br>than iPhone X |

iPhone XS looks more appropriate for those that admire and loved using a portable size of iPhone, but to some that appreciate the big size of the iPhone that will make their fingers open and free to move around when tapping during or selecting closed options and typing text/passcode from a keyboard or dialing contact on Keypad…and many others, they are good to go for iPhone XS Max.

In some cases, some individuals would go for iPhone XS Max because of their big fingers, large view of the screen display, and increase in battery power duration while some will choose iPhone XS over iPhone XS Max because of their portable fingers and less weight of the iPhone XS.

Now let's come to look into the different parts of the iPhone from the backside which is also called the rear side of the iPhone and the other important surrounding parts that include sides and front operational tools that can help you to fully enjoy your iPhone.

**Rear (Back) Cameras:** These are the two cameras at the back of your iPhone 11:

1.  12MP Wide Camera with a small focus of depth field f/1.8 aperture.
2.  12MP Ultra Wide Camera of a small focus of depth field f/2.4 aperture.

The two cameras can stabilize optical image with Photograph Next-generation Smart HDR that overcome night interference with the use of Night mode. The rear cameras are efficient to record QuickTake video.

**The Screen Display**

The screen display is made up of Super Retinal High Dynamic Rate Display of 5.8 inches diagonal screen Organic Light-Emitting Diode (OLED) Multi-Touch size in iPhone XS while the iPhone XS Max full-screen OLED Multi-Touch Display is 6.5 Inches.

OLED, as the name implies, is a natural component of Carbon compound that produces light which is vision friendly light to human eyes still you should use Night Shift mode if you are having sight defect to protect and improve your eyes health.

You will fully learn how to turn On Night Mode in the control center and other ways of controlling screen light latter in this iPhone User Manual.

The OLED display enables advanced contrast and penetration of highly dark backgrounds that show all compressed hidden images in the background.

It also helps in separating close white appearance of images with their white or transparent background.

iPhone XS has a resolution capacity of 2,436 by 1,125-pixel resolution at a rate of 458 pixels per inch (PPI) while iPhone XS Max has a resolution ability of 2,688 by 1,242-pixel resolution at the same rate of iPhone XS.

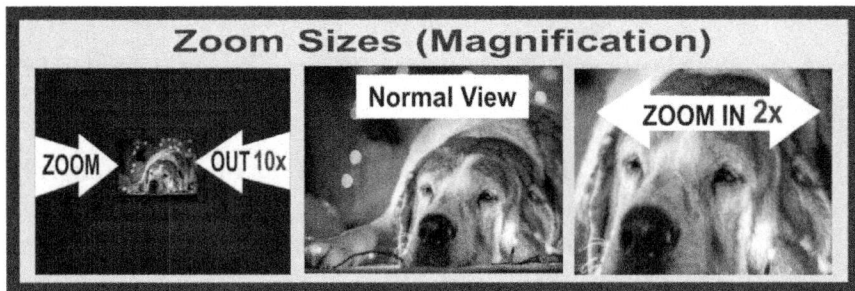

**Zoom Magnification:** You can zoom out optical images to 10 times (10x) of the original image on your camera screen and digitally zoom in the image up to 2 times (2x) of the original image on the iPhone. You can also perform Audio Zoom as an innovation in the iPhone generation without losing the image quality.

**Portrait Mode:** The Portrait effect in the Camera capture help with the use of advanced Bokeh and Depth Control to produce Portrait Mode that can further use Filter and 5 Portrait Lighting Effects which include Natural, Studio, Contour, Stage, and Stage Mono.

**Audio Playback:** You can effectively use the iPhone to make Audio Playback with supported Dolby Atoms and Spatial Audio Playback.

**Video Playback:** The iPhone can be appropriately used with supported HDR10 Content and Dolby Vision

**What Your iPhone Notch Has and What The Components Do**

A notch is a black compartment at the top center of the iPhone that contains many **Sensors** like *Infrared Sensor, Flood Illuminator, Proximity Sensor and Ambient Light Sensor*; **Microphone, Speaker, 7MP Front-Facing Camera of depth field   f/2.2 aperture, and Dot Projector**.

iPhone XS & XS Max Notch Components

Infrared
Flood Illuminator
Proximity Sensor
Ambient Light Sensor
Dot Projector
7MP Front-Facing Camera
Microphone
Speaker

**The Microphone** will help to improve your voice when you are making a call or voice recording. The microphone can also be seen at the back of the iPhone by the sides of the flash and the bottom of the iPhone.

**The Speaker** will help you hear a loud sound and clear through the out-speaker. You may listen to the audio, voice without using ear-pieces or earphones or headphones. Speaker can also be found at the left and right side of the lightning port of the iPhone bottom.

**7MP Front-Facing Camera** could quickly enable you to take selfies while the camera at the front of your iPhone which is called the *Front-Facing Camera*. It comes with TrueDepth of 7MP of a

13

small focus of depth field f/2.2 aperture with a resolution of 1080p HD for video recording and picture capture.

**A12 Bionic Chip Capacity:** It comes with A12 Bionic Chip of Second Generation Natural Engine that is boosted with an in-built internal *Random Access Memory* of 4 GB to improve the operational functions of the iPhone in term of uploading, execution of various tasks which include setup, video recording, sending or receiving of messages, downloading of video, performing of transaction… and many others.

**Different Memory Storage Capacity:** iPhone XS and XS Max come with different storage capacities of 64 GB and 128 GB (Gigabyte) that determine the price of the iPhone XS and XS Max. The storage capacity is the space that is naturally available on your iPhone. The more the space capacity you have on your iPhone the more data or documents you can store on your iPhone storage. Therefore, if you go for iPhone XS or XS Max with high storage capacity you will have an opportunity to have more data or documents on your iPhone XS, however, you can still support your iPhone Storage with iCloud Storage to backup all your data and apps on your iPhone XS and XS Max.

**Battery Durability:** iPhone XS and XS Max have the same strength capacity of 2,658mAh – Lion of 3.81 Voltage (V) and 3.80V that can enable you to perform longer activities. iPhone XS is 2hours 30 minutes stronger than iPhone 7 while iPhone XS Max is 1hour stronger than iPhone XS. On many occasions, the rate of battery discharged depends on the time (duration) of different activities you are doing on your iPhone. If you are doing many functions or you are using the iPhone for a longer time than normal it may reduce the time of the battery.

**How You Can Protect Your iPhone Battery Life Span:**

1. When you have fully charged your iPhone XS or XS Max battery, remove it from the source of light before you start operating the iPhone.
2. Ensure you have used the battery to 50-40% charged before you connect your iPhone to the source of electricity for recharge.
3. Always avoid your iPhone XS or XS Max battery from being completely discharged or rundown to 5 or 0% before you recharge it.
4. Do not allow the iPhone XS or XS Max to suddenly trip off because the battery has been discharged totally.
5. Set battery percentage limit and battery protective move on your iPhone to provide your iPhone longer time of using it.
6. If you want to carry out a setup or uploading or downloading or recording that will take too much of time that the current battery level cannot complete, immediately, connect it to the source of electricity to boost the battery capacity and once it is fully charged then disconnect the iPhone from the USB lightning cable and continue your activity.

**How You Can Connect Lightning to USB Cable and Adapter to Charge iPhone XS**

In the package of the iPhone XS, you will see a Lightning to USB Cable, an Adapter of 18 Watt, a Pair of Earpod with a connecting cable, and a SIM Card Tray Ejector.

**First Step:** Take the first end of the lightning to USB Cable and insert it into the iPhone Power Port under the bottom of the iPhone XS and XS Max.

Speaker & In Built Microphone

iPhone XS

Speaker & In Built Microphone

iPhone XS Max

First End

Power Port
Power Connector

Lightning to USB Cable

Second End

USB Adpter Connector

USB Adpter

**Second Step:** Take the second end of the lightning to USB Cable and insert the USB connector into the USB lightning adapter port at the head of the Adapter.

**Third Step:** Plug the USB Adapter pins inside an electric Plug socket and switch on the button of the plug.

**Hint:** Within a few seconds charging batteries with the percentage charged will show on the screen for you to know that the iPhone XS or XS Max is effectively

53% Charged

charging. But, if you waited for about a minute without you seeing the battery charging icon came up, adjust the adapter connected with the main plug of the source of electricity.

## The iPhone XS & SX Max Side Buttons

Right Side  Left Side

Silence Button

Up Volume Button

Down Volume Button

Power/Switch /Siri Button

The iPhone XS and iPhone XS Max have their external operational buttons in the same location as the iPhone. At the left side of the iPhone you will see:

1. The Silence Button.
2. The Up Volume Button
3. The Down Volume Button.

On the right side of the

iPhone, you will see the Power Switch or Siri Button that can be used to turn ON the iPhone.

## The Wireless and Cellular That Can Work With Your iPhone XS or XS Max

The iPhone can use EDGE or GSM, DC-HSPA+, LITE Advanced, HSPA+, or UMTS, few models of CDMA EV-DO Rev. A, Bluetooth 5.0, Express Cards, In-Built of GNSS or GPS, 802.11ac Wi-Fi with MIMO, and NFC with reader mode.

**IP68 Certification:** iPhone XS has just a 30-minute resistant ability to endure 1 meter of water depth. It is not advisable to deliberately put your iPhone XS in water that you do not know the depth of the water. It is only satisfied with the 1-meter depth of water not more than that. More also, iPhone XS can survive in a dusty environment.

## Documents You Can Access on Your iPhone XS

There documents you access on your iPhone XS without looking for a format converter. Any of the accepted documents can be used or shared on the website page, mail, social media platform or to compose a message on your iPhone as a reminder or planner… and many others.

The documents are:

1. Microsoft Excel of XISX and XIS
2. Microsoft PowerPoint of PPTX
3. Microsoft Word of DOCX and DOC
4. Text of TXT
5. Image of JPG, GIF, TIFF;
6. USDZ Universal of USDZ, ZIP, and ICS
7. Keynote of KEY
8. Preview and Adobe Acrobat Document Format of PDF
9. Contact information of VCF
10. Rich Text Format or RTF
11. Numbers of NUMBERS format.

# Correct Method of Putting SIM Card into Your iPhone

Your iPhone XS or XS Max does not support **Micro-SIM Cards.**

How You Can Put In SIM Card Into Your iPhone XS & XS Max

Front Side

SIM Card Compartment

SIM Card Compartment

Ejector Hole

SIM Card Tray    Back Side

SIM Card Front

SIM Tray Cover

SIM Tray Ejector

Parallel/Horizontal Position

You can use Nano-SIM and eSIM (Dual SIM) on your iPhone XS or XS Max. There is a **SIM Tray Ejector** in the iPhone XS or XS Max pack that you will use to eject the SIM Card tray from the right-hand side of the iPhone below the Power Button.

**First Step**: Let the front of your iPhone XS or XS Max face up; with your hand pick Ejector and position it to be parallel/horizontal to the hole at the lower end of the SIM Card tray's cover.

**Second Step**: Insert the SIM Ejector into the small hole to touch the end surface inside and push the surface, immediately the SIM Card tray will partially come out.

**Third Step:** Use your hand to pull it out completely.

**Fourth Step:** Let the Circuit Steel surface (the front face) of your SIM Card face up and place the card on the tray according to the shape of the SIM. **Do not position the SIM card against the shape designed on the SIM Tray. Do not turn the SIM face upside down.**

**Fifth Step:** Insert the SIM Tray with SIM Card on it back to the SIM compartment as you removed it. Now you are through.

**How You Can Solve Problems on Your iPhone**

The pages that you will need to access to get to where you are going on your iPhone were written in **bold font** with red color to call your attention.

After you have tapped on any app like the Settings app on the **Homescreen** you will see the next action you will tap in Bold Black font. If you are to further from their then you will see the first bold black word that will be written bold red font on the second line and the next action will be written bold black font.

Each bold red word represented each page title that you will see at the top of the screen page during settings.

For example, you are going to Camera Settings.

Homescreen: Hit on the **Setting Icon** (First Line of Action).

Settings: Scroll down to select **Camera** (Second Line of Action).

On the first line of action, you will see Homescreen appears in red color which means the name of the screen page, while **Settings Icon** appears in black which means "what you are looking for on the page (i.e. your mission)".

On the second line of action, the **Settings Icon** changes to Settings because at this stage you have launched the Settings page, therefore, the red color appearance of Settings is representing the Settings page not "mission", while **Camera** is your next mission on the Settings page.

## Meaning of Terms

Please get used to the meaning of the below simple terms that I used in this book to help you learn and digest different technical steps quickly.

**Hit** or **Select**: This means **"Tap"**. Whenever you see hit on a particular **application** or **feature**, I mean you should tap on the app or the feature.

**Activator:** It is used for the "switch button" to turn on apps features in Settings.       or

**Activate:** This means you should turn on the **Activator.**

**Deactivate:** This means you should turn off the **Activator.**

**Regulator:** It means **"Control"**. It has a round slider on a parallel line that can be moved to either right or left to regulate the level of volume of a sound or light on your iPhone XS Settings.

**Type:** It means "Enter" words or numbers into a text or searches filed.

**Text or Search Field**: This is a place where you can type in words or numbers.

**Rotator**: It is the Icon used to turn the camera view from either back(rear)-facing camera to the front-facing camera to take a Selfie or from the front camera to the back camera to take video or pictures.

# GUIDE ONE

## Why You Need to Upgrade iOS & Important Applications (Apps)

### *What is the importance of Upgraded iOS?*

iOS is fully called the iPhone Operating System. It is a software programming that enables the iPhone to perform all the various features that you can benefits on the iPhone through the manual or automatic setup and installation of all the important applications (Apps) that will enable you to do what you want to do on the iPhone with ease.

The number at the end of the iOS e.g. iOS **12** determines the level of innovativeness and benefits you can find in the iPhone running with iOS 12. When iPhone is upgraded to upper iOS 13 you will enjoy more inventions and advancement that come with the iOS.

Some of the benefits are the increase in efficiency and speed to upload, download, video recording, setup, transfer of data, browse, and quick navigation.

You can also enjoy newly introduced customized Animoji, different health apps navigating steps, and recovery of your lost iPhone even when your iPhone battery is down… and many others.

When you upgrade your iPhone XS or XS Max to the latest version of iOS 13.1 above you will equally benefit everything in iPhone 11, 11 Pro, and 11 Pro Max. Instead of ignoring or selling your current iPhone XS or XS Max for iPhone 11 and others that come with iOS 13, you can better upgrade your iPhone XS iOS to the latest version running in the iPhone products 2019.

# The Importance of Applications (Apps)

Application on your iPhone XS or XS Max is designed to perform different functions. As the name implies Application, this is a tool you can apply on your iPhone to carry out many activities that are related to its functions.

For example Camera App, in this Camera Application, you can record videos, take photos, and edit them for future use. This means that in Camera App is a tool that contains different sub-tools or equipment that will enable you to record video, take photos and make them come out pretty good for you to use them for another purpose like Personal Photo, Profile Picture, Wallpaper, Media Presentation, or Video Watch... and many others.

For every iPhone user to quickly recognize all the available Apps on iPhone XS and XS Max, Apps are given different designed **Icons** to represent them. It is on these Icons that a user will tap to see the features inside the apps and what they are capable of doing. Camera App is represented with Camera Image as Icon.

**How Apps Works**

By default, several App will be automatically installed after the setup but before you can benefit all the advance features you need to put On their activation switch in the **Settings App**.

This will be fully discussed later in this iPhone XS or XS Max Manual.

**What are the Icons on iPhone XS or XS Max Screens?**

The major screens of your iPhone are:

1. **Lock Screen**
2. **Home Screen**

## Lock Screen

This is the primary entry screen that contains a timer, date, notifications, camera icon, cellular icon, Wi-Fi network icon, battery icon, flash icon, and security lock icon.

The most important features of the icons on the Lock screen are:

Cellular Icon: The icon is showing the level of network service on your iPhone. The three inclined vertical bars show the strength of the network on your iPhone wherever you are.

iPhone XS & XS Max Lock Screen

LTE: When you see LTE on your iPhone XS or XS Max top this shows that at the location you are there is a strong network that can make your activity on the internet to be very faster on your 3G and 4G iPhone.

3G & 4G: Your iPhone is designed to use 3G SIM and 4G SIM cellular networks. The 4G network is more efficient and faster than 3G SIM cellular network.

Wi-Fi: This is an internet browsing network that makes use of data to upload, download, update, or transfer documents; and to connect Android, Apple Watch, or iPhone to your iPhone XS. The Icon can be found beside the cellular icon at the top right of the iPhone. You will read more later in this Manual.

Battery Icon: This is showing the level of battery charged on your iPhone. If the battery is going down the level of the battery will be reduced from the top to the bottom of the battery. The icon is at the top right of the iPhone. You will read more later.

23

**Lock Icon:** When the Padlock is open it shows that the iPhone is open but when it remains locked that means that the Lock Screen is still locked.

**Timer:** It automatically set itself with the most accurate regional global time of your location. It instantly determines regional timing.

**Notifications:** It strictly works by your instruction to provide you alert information that will be shown on the Lock screen.

But, by default, it would display all information about missed calls, alarm, received emails, messages notification. However, you may avoid your messages or mail details from showing on the Lock screen through notification settings; to prevent anyone from viewing your privacy.

**You have to unlock your iPhone before you can perform the following:**

**Flash:** You can use the flash at the bottom left of the Lock screen to lightening the dark environment and facilitates sharp and clear output of pictures taking in uniformly dark surroundings.

**Camera:** It can be constantly used to perform video coverage, and pictures taking without you navigating through the Homescreen.

Also, you could swipe from the right side of the iPhone to launch the Camera page or press the Switch button to access Camera and click on any of the **down or up volume** buttons at the left side of the iPhone to take a picture if you don't want to use Shutter at the bottom center of the Camera screen.

**Apps Searching Tool:** When you slide your iPhone from the left side you will see searching tools that will enable you to find many apps information on your iPhone. Ask more of Apple store, iCloud, or Siri to know more about them. There is much informative news that is displaced below that you can hit on to read more if your Wi-Fi network is On.

Place your finger at the bottom of the Notch frame center of your iPhone and slightly move down your finger you will see a searching field with suggested favorite Apps that you can navigate to get what you need on the iPhone.

But, if that app you are looking for is not among the suggested apps, you can further type in the app into the searching field to access the app.

Hint: Whenever you see **Search or Text Field** on your iPhone without seeing any Keyboard to type text into the field. All you need to do is to initially hit on the surface of the **Search or Text field**, immediately Keyboard will appear below for you to enter your search text keywords into the field. Examples of apps that contain text field are Mail, Messages, Safari, or other Browsers, Camera, Call Contact, Calendar, FaceTime, Health… and many others.

Control Center: You can view Control Center from the Lock screen. Swipe down from the top right side of the Notch on your iPhone.

The security padlock will be unlocked through your **Face Identity (ID)** if you have done the Face ID during the iPhone Setup. A blinking infra-red sensor will be showing from the **Notch** at the top center of your iPhone and once you look at the Lock screen, your face will be scanned and the locked padlock will open for you to access the Home screen by swiping up from the bottom center of the screen.

**Home Screen**

This is the second screen that also contained a timer, cellular icon, Wi-Fi network icon, battery icon, and all the Apps that I have mentioned above.

The Apps occupy two screen pages that you can see when you swipe the Home screen from right to left.

**iPhone XS & XS Max Homescreen**

All the available Apps' Icons on the iPhone XS Home screen that has been upgraded from iOS 12 to iOS 13 are stated below:

Messages, 9

Calendar, Photos, Camera, Weather, Clock, Maps, FaceTime, Notes,

Reminder, Stocks, News, Home, iTune Store, Apple Store, Books, Health, Wallet, Settings, Podcast, Phone, Mail, Safari, Music, Find My, Shortcuts, Contacts, Compass, Measure, Calculator, Files, Watch, and Tips.

You can still request more apps on your iPhone through Apple Store freely. More apps you can get from the Apple store are iMovie, iTunes Remote, iTunes U, Number, GarageBand, Clips, Keynote, Pages, and Music Memos.

All the above apps are very important for you to fully benefit the operational efficiency of your iPhone and make life very simple to explore and achievable. **The most important and inevitable Apps that you must know the beneficial features are Settings, Call, Messages, Camera, Photo, FaceTime, Siri, Safari, Mail, Music, Find My, and Health.**

**Settings:** This app will enable you to access the settings of all the available apps on your iPhone. Through the Settings app, you can perfectly activate all the essential apps (e.g. Face ID, Siri, Passcode, Wi-Fi Network, iCloud, etc.) that you are unable or skipped during your iPhone setup.

**Phone:** This will enable you to reach out to your friends or loved ones that you are having their **contact** details on your iPhone. The phone app will enable you to receive or make a call.

**Massage:** This will enable you to send text messages to your loved ones in your contacts. You have two ways of sending a message to people.

1. SMS or MMS
2. iMessage

SMS or MMS: You can send a text message through SMS and MMS to anyone on your contact that is using an Android phone. The sending button is green

iMessage: This is a live interactive message medium that will enable you to see when the person you are sending your text message to is typing his/her messages. It is only available for those who are using an iPhone. The sending icon is blue.

**Camera:** This will enable you to take new pictures or images and record videos of any event. In it, there is image beatifying features that can be applied to edit and modify the image output.

**Photos:** In this app, you can fully access all your saved pictures regarding time, day, month, location, and event. This app will arrange and indicate the source of store images such as *Screenshot, WhatsApp, Facebook, Video, Movies, DCIM, Camera, Live Pictures...and others.* You can add labels to any specific event photographs.

**FaceTime:** As the name of the app implies **FaceTime,** it will enable you to make face to face calls, audio calls, live to chat text messages on your iPhone with the use of the latest Animoji or customized, Memoji and Emoji.

**Siri:** This app is a wonderful work-executor and apps, problem solver. It serves as a messenger or personal assistant to help you determine several activities associated with other apps on your iPhone. It can help you set and save time in Alarm, a reminder for events, check daily weather/climatic condition, recall the missed calls or messages and it can also help you compose messages and send to whosoever you want to send it to.

If you call its attention, it will do anything you want it to do for you. Its voice could be set to female or male voice all depends on your choice. It is one of the great successes ever apple has achieved in using technology to solve the iPhone user's bothering issues with ease.

**Safari:** This app is used to browse for any information online or to download more applications, games, dictionaries, music, videos, language translator, WhatsApp, Facebook... and many others.

**Mail:** The App will enable you to instantly access your received email messages and to reply to messages.

**Music:** This app will enable you to play any audio music in your music library.

**Health:** This is an amazing app that you can use to track everything about your health to ensure your daily general wellbeing. You can also use it to monitor your daily food consumption through the regulation of calories and monthly menstrual cycle in women; heart condition, fasting discipline, sleeping status, working ability... and many other activities essential to your comfortable life.

**Find My:** This is App very important to either quickly use to locate your misplaced iPhone or retrieve suspected lost iPhone without using a Wi-Fi network or Cellular connection even when the battery is done you can still recover your lost iPhone.

# *How You Could Upgrade iOS 12 on Your iPhone XS to Latest iOS 13 Version*

It is of great advantage to upgrading the current iOS 12 on your iPhone XS or XS Max to the latest version of iOS 13 for you to benefit more of the latest features loaded in other advance iPhones like iPhone 11, 11 Pro, 11 Pro Max, and Second Generation iPhone SE using iOS 13 with high-speed efficiency.

**Things You Must Put In Place Before You Start**
- ➢ Get an effective Wi-Fi network.
- ➢ Confirm the available storage space on your iPhone XS. If you do not have up to 90 GB you can purchase from the iCloud store for more storage.
- ➢ Use iCloud or Mac or PC to back up all the data and documents on your iPhone.
- ➢ Charge your iPhone, and Mac or PC. You may connect your iPhone or upgrading device to a power source overnight.
- ➢ Make your Password available.
- ➢ Good lightning to USB cord.

**How to perform Backup and iOS Upgrade on Computer**

The Operational System for Apple Macintosh Computer (Mac)

- ➢ macOS Catalina 10.15 or
- ➢ macOS Mojave 10.14 or lower version.

Note: You may use a PC if you do not have Mac.

If your Mac is running with a low version of macOS Mojave you can quickly update your Mac by taking the following step on your Mac.

29

**On App Menu:**

➢ Select **System Preferences** (operating system).
➢ Click on **Software Update** to look for an Updates
➢ Click on the **Update Now** option to install the latest version benefits. If you select **More Info** you will see full information on the individual update and later choose the one you preferred.
➢ Leave it for a while to completely install till you will see a message that "**your software is up to date**.

Now you can confidently move on to the update process of your iPhone XS on your newly updated Mac.

**Step by Step of iPhone XS Update on macOS Catalina 10.15**

➢ Put On your Mac.
➢ Put On the Wi-Fi network connection on your Mac or PC

➢ Launch **Finder**

But if you are using a Mac

Where To Locate Your iPhone XS or XS Max On Computer

**Finder** (macOS Catalina)

Favorites

**Locations**

iPhone XS

**iTunes 12** (macOS Mojave or PC)

Music

iPhone XS

100%

**iTunes 11** (macOS Mojave or PC)

Search Library

hone ≡ iTunes Store

**iTunes 10** (macOS Mojave or PC)

DEVICES

hone

Music

Movies

TV Shows

30

running with macOS Mojave 10.14 or less, you will open **iTunes**

## Step by Step of iPhone XS Update on macOS Catalina 10.15

➢ Use the lightning to USB Cable to connect your iPhone XS with Mac USB port. 

➢ Look at the left side of the Finder page you will see the image of your iPhone and the iPhone name under **Location.**

- (If you have signed up your name with Apple ID, your first name will appear at the front of the iPhone image). Hit on the name of your iPhone.
- The location at which you can locate your iPhone differents from the iTunes version to another iTunes version in macOS Mojave and PC.
- However, the location of your iPhone XS or XS Max on iTunes 10 – 12 was shown on the screenshot below.

➢ Once you click on your iPhone XS or XS Max the Update provisional page for your iPhone will display at the right-hand side.

➢ Initially click on **Backup all the data on your iPhone to this Mac.**

➢ Click **Check for Update.**

➢ Click **Download** and **Update.**

➢ When you are asked to provide your **Passcode,** immediately type your **Passcode.**

The update will start, endure until the update is complete.

Do not interrupt the update processing.

## How to perform iOS Update on your New iPhone XS

Homescreen:

➢ Place your finger at the top right of the iPhone screen and swipe down to launch **Control Center.**

➢ Hit on Cellular Service and Wi-Fi network.

> Swipe up from the bottom or hit the down plain of the screen to return to Homescreen.

> Hit on **Settings Icon.**

Settings: Scroll down to hit on **General**

General: Hit on **Software Update.**

Software Update: Select **Download** and **Install**

If your passcode is required then continue by:

Passcode: Type the correct **Passcode.**

Terms and Conditions: Select **Agree** at the lower left to progress but if you mistakenly select **Disagree** it will discontinue the upgrade.

Immediately, the Upgrade will start, and you can let the iPhone upgrade overnight to finish the general processing because it always takes much time.

# GUIDE TWO

## How You Can Make Your iPhone XS/XS Max To Start Working After Manual Setup

Beginners need to get all the necessary things that will enable them to successfully setup XS or XS Max without any problem. If you are using Android before you bought iPhone XS or XS Max and now you needed to move all your significant documents or information to your new iPhone, you can do the transfer during the manual setup or after you have successfully done the setup.

However, in the event that you need to move during the setup, you have to turn On the Wi-Fi network on your Android Phone that you will accept on your iPhone. However, it is more advisable you initially finish your iPhone XS or XS Max setup before you transfer from Android to your new iPhone.

Because you will have a high chance of great success in transferring your documents or data by using your iPhone Wi-Fi network to drive the files.

You may need to enable Bluetooth on your iPhone XS or XS Max at the control center. All these will help you to transfer your data and documents on the Android phone without any problem.

All the steps you will need to do for you to easily move documents or data from Android to your new iPhone XS or XS Max were fully discussed after the "Automatic Setup of iPhone" in this Guide Two.

### *What To Do First*

➢ When you removed the iPhone XS or XS Max from the sealed pack, connect the lightning to USB cord to the power port at the under bottom center of the iPhone.

- Connect the other USB end to 18 Watt USB port adapter at the head and plug it to the electric source to charge the iPhone.
- If you are having Computer, you can connect the USD connector of the cable to your fully charge Computer USB port.
- On the iPhone screen, the current battery charged will appear. Once it is fully charged disconnect your XS or XS Max from the source of electricity.
- Insert your SIM card according to the method you have been told earlier.
- Protect the iPhone with a nice iPhone XS or XS Max case and screen protector as being discussed in the Bonus Guide in the last part of this manual book.

**Do you have videos, audio music or messages, photos, or any other essential documents you want to transfer from your Personal Computer or Android Phone?**
- Turn On the Wi-Fi network on your Android or PC containing the data or documents you wanted to transfer into your new XS or XS Max.
- Rename the Wi-Fi ID on your Android or Computer Wi-Fi settings to ease the Wi-Fi name recognition of your XS or XS Max. (Optional).
- Endure the Network is active and the Android or PC is fully charged.

Now you can take a further step of performing a fully manual setup of your newly purchased iPhone XS or XS Max.

1. Power Switch Button
   Look at the right side of the new iPhone you will see a button, Press down till you will see a big **Hello** font interpreting in different languages on the screen
2. Hello
   Swipe up from the bottom center to tap on your **Language**.

3. Select Your Country or Region

34

Scroll down to tap on your **Country.**

4. **Quick Start**
   Look down the screen hit on **Set Up Manually.**

5. **Choose a Wi-Fi Network**
   Hit on the name of your **Wi-Fi Source.**

6. **Enter Password**
   Enter the correct password of the **Wi-Fi Network** and tap on **Join** at the top right side of the screen.

7. **Data & Privacy**
   Hit the **Continue** bar

8. **Face ID**
   a. Hit on the **Continue** bar.
   b. Hit on **"Get Started"** bar
   c. Focus your eyes on the Front-Facing Camera Sensor and let your head be in the middle of the round frame on the screen.
   d. As you are turning your head gradually the surrounding lines of the round frame will be changing to green, keep turning your head and let every side of

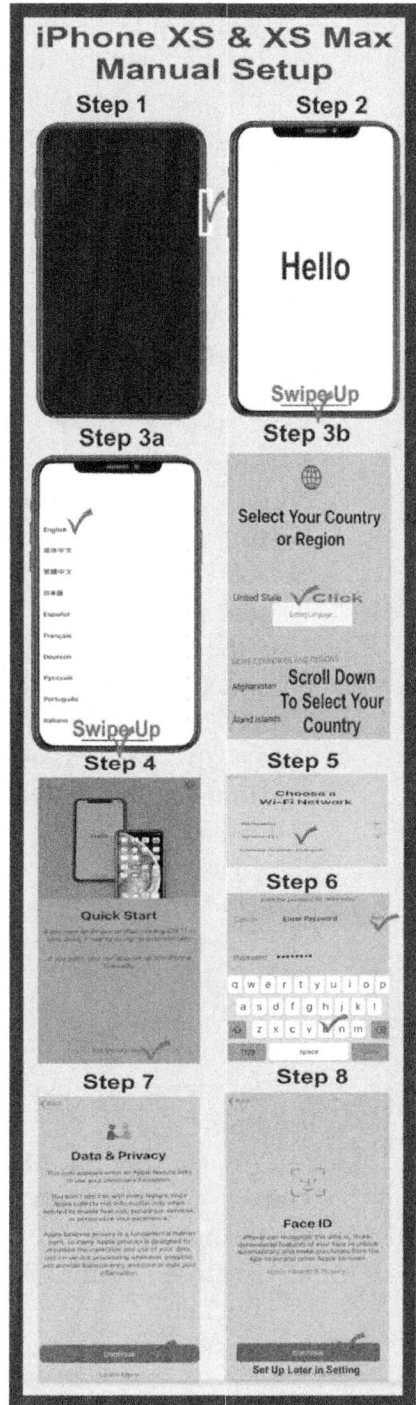

iPhone XS & XS Max Manual Setup

Step 1    Step 2

Hello

Swipe Up

Step 3a    Step 3b

Select Your Country or Region

Scroll Down To Select Your Country

Step 4    Step 5

Swipe Up

Choose a Wi-Fi Network

Quick Start    Step 6

Enter Password

Step 7    Step 8

Data & Privacy

Face ID

Set Up Later in Setting

35

your head be captured by the Camera sensor till the surrounding lines are completely changed to green.

e. If the Face ID is successful, a **Continue** page will display. Hit the **Continue** bar.

9. For **later Face ID Settings** hit the second option **Set Up Later in Settings.**

10. Create a Passcode
Use the Keypad to type complex **Passcode.** But, if you are not prepared, then tap on **Passcode Options** and hit on **Don't Use Passcode.**

11. Passcode Box
Hit on **Don't Use Passcode.**

12. Apps & Data
If you are having data on Android Phone you can hit on the option **Move Data from Android. Other options**
a. Restore from iCloud Backup
b. Restore from Mac or PC

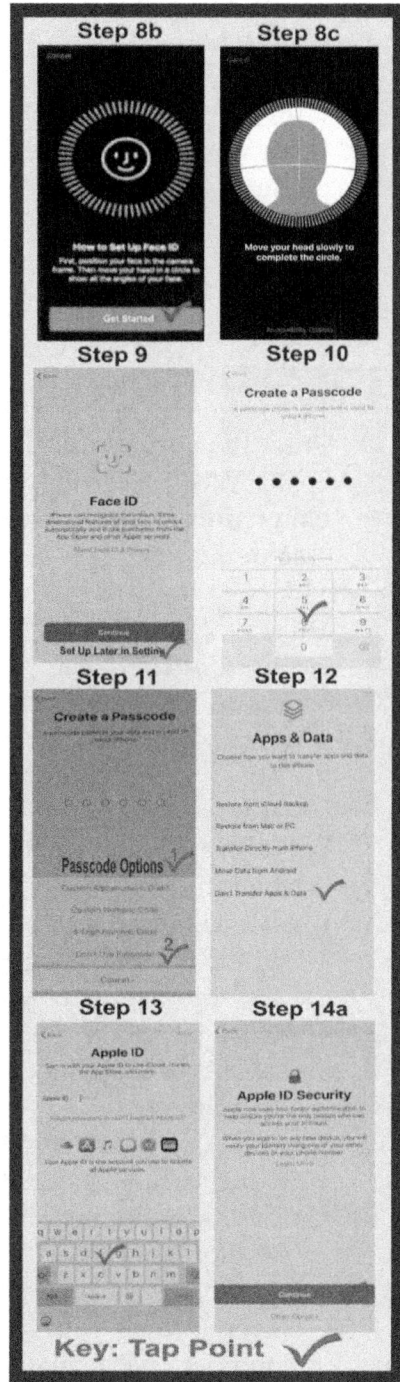

36

c. Don't Transfer Apps & Data

13. **Apple ID**
    a. Tap on the Text Field, use the Keyboard to type your Email address
    b. Hit on **Next** at the top right angle side.
    c. Type a correct **Apple Password** inside the text field.
    d. Hit on **Next** at the top right side of the screen.

14. **Apple ID Security**
    Hit the **Continue** bar to register your **Phone Number.**
    But, if do not want that to be done during setup then you can tap on **Other Options**
    Hit on **Don't Upgrade** on the **Request Box.**

15. **Terms and Condition**
    Read and digest the terms and conditions for you to know how you could successfully use your iPhone and follow them strictly. Tap on the **Agree** option at the bottom right of the screen.

16. **Express Settings**
    Hit **Continue** bar below

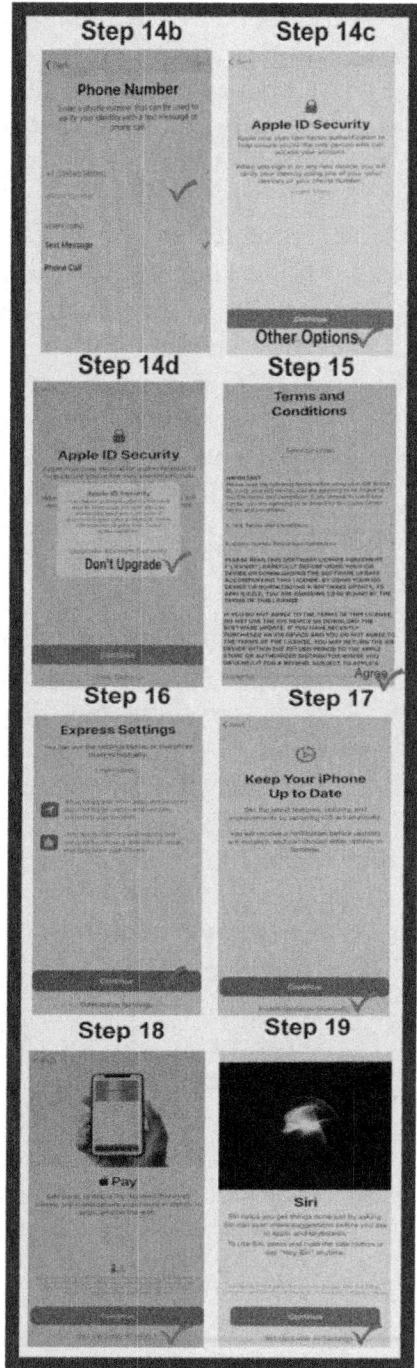

37

17. **Keep Your iPhone Up to Date**
Choose the below option of **Install Update Manually.**

18. **Apple Pay**
Enter your Apple Wallet detail if it is available with you by hitting on **Continue** bar.
But, choose **Set Up Later in Wallet** option below, if you don't have or ready for it.

19. **Siri**
Tap on **Continue** bar to register Siri (optional)
But, tap on **Set Up Later in Settings** to perform the full settings of Siri through the Settings process.

20. **Screen Timer**
Hit **Continue** bar (optional), it could be done later, therefore, for now, choose **Set Up Later in Settings.**

21. **Apple Analytics**
Select the **Don't Share** option below Share with App Developers.

22. **True Tone Display**

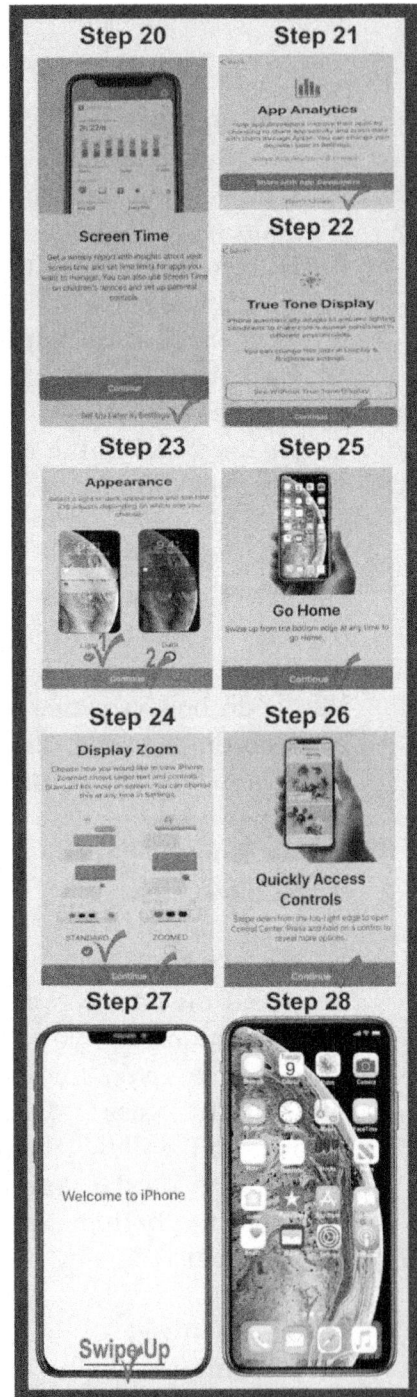

38

Hit on **Continue** bar

23. Appearance
    a. Select on **Light** option to make the iPhone screen appear brighter.
    b. Hit **Continue** bar

24. Display Zoom
    Hit **Standard** small circle to select it.
    Hit **Continue** bar

25. Go Home
    Hit **Continue** bar

26. Switch Between Recent Apps
    Hit **Continue** bar

27. Quickly Access Controls
    Hit **Continue** bar

28. Welcome to iPhone
    Swipe up from the bottom middle of the screen to access the **Homepage.** If you create a Passcode during setup, the iPhone will ask you to enter your registered Passcode before you can launch into the Homescreen.

# *How You Can Transfer Data or Documents from Old iPhone to iPhone XS or XS Max Automatically*

**Things that may affect the automatic transfer**

✓ Off Bluetooth or Bad Rear Camera Sensor
✓ Poor Cellular connection or Wi-Fi Network
✓ Entering of Incorrect Apple ID
✓ Activation of "*Find My iPhone*" Settings.
✓ Low Charged Battery

✓ Insufficient storage space on new iPhone XS or XS Max

**What You Must Do On Your Old iPhone**

✓ Recharged your iPhone Battery
✓ Enable Bluetooth
✓ Enable Cellular connection & Wi-Fi Network
✓ Enable "*Find My iPhone*" Settings.
✓ Ensure you enter the correct Apple ID when it is needed.

**How You Can Enable Hotspot and Enter Wi-Fi Password on Old iPhone**

There is a need for some little steps of apps' activations through settings on your old iPhone before you move all the data and documents into the new iPhone XS or XS Max.

The first things to do on your old iPhone are:

➤ Go to Control Center on your iPhone, tap on the Cellular Service icon, Wi-Fi icon, and Bluetooth icon to turn them on.

If the Wi-Fi network is not responding or you have not turned on the Wi-Fi connection on your old iPhone before, then do the following step to activate your old iPhone Personal Hotspot.

Homescreen: Tap on Settings Button

Settings Page: Tap on Personal Hotspot

Hotspot Page:

1. Hit on **Personal Hotspot** activation switch to turn green.
2. On the dialog box, Wi-Fi and Bluetooth are Off, then tap on **Turn On Wi-Fi and Bluetooth.**
3. On displayed Bluetooth Off Dialog Box tap on **Wi-Fi and USB Only.**

**4.** Hit on **Wi-Fi Password**

## Wi-Fi Password:

1. Hit on the **Password Text Field surface** and use the keyboard below on the page to enter your **"Wi-Fi Password"**.

2. Hit on **Done** at the top angle of the iPhone.

3. Hit on the Home button to return to Homescreen.
   But, if your old iPhone is iPhone X then swipe up from the bottom center.

Now that the old iPhone Wi-Fi Network, Cellular Service, and Bluetooth were turned on and active, you can move to the next stage of moving data from the old iPhone to your new iPhone XS or XS Max.

How to Enable Hotspot on Old iPhone

41

**Do you have videos, audio music or messages, photos, or any other essential documents you want to transfer from your Personal Computer or Android Phone?**

➢ Turn On the Wi-Fi network on your Android or PC containing the data or documents you wanted to transfer into your new iPhone XS or XS Max. (If you have initially set up your iPhone manually, use your iPhone Wi-Fi network instead).

➢ Rename the Wi-Fi ID on your Android or Computer Wi-Fi settings to ease the recognition on your iPhone XS or XS Max. (Optional).

➢ Endure the Network is active and the Android or PC is fully charged.

## *How To Place Old iPhone and New iPhone*

The old iPhone could either be placed on the right side of the new iPhone or the left side of the new iPhone, however, what is significant is that they ought not to be excessively far from each other.

On the off chance that you are a lefty/left hand using person, you could place the new iPhone at the left side of the old iPhone.

In any case, if you are a righty/right hand using person, place the new iPhone at the right side of the old iPhone because you will perform more installation tasks on the new iPhone than the old iPhone.

Make sure that the distance is 2 to 3cm between each of them.

You may put your SIM card later but make sure the battery is 100% charged before you start.

In this cool guide, I transferred data and apps from iPhone 6 running with iOS 11 to my newly purchased iPhone XS.

Hint: You must upgrade your old iPhone iOS to 11 to enable the transfer of the data and document.

## *How You Can Back-up Everything on Your Old iPhone Before Automatic Transfer*

Save all your data with iCloud secure storage backup by navigating through:

Homescreen – Hit on the **Settings** icon

Settings – Hit on your **Name Profile** to access Apple ID.

Apple ID – Hit on **iCloud**

iCloud – Search downward and hit the **iCloud Backup** activation button to put on the iCloud Backup.

Backup – Hit on **Back Up Now** to start the iCloud Backup.

Home Button – Click on the round Home Button down to go back to the Home screen, if you are using iPhone X swipe up for Home screen. Now you can start the setup process below.

Automatic Setup & Data Transfer
Step 1

Switch On

Step 2 & 3
Hello
Swipe Up Step 2
Swipe Up Step 3

Step 4a
Waiting for your iPhone...
Let Rear Camera Focus

Step 4b
Waiting for Other iPhone...

Step 5
Enter Passcode of Your Other iPhone

Step 6a
Face ID

Key: Where to Tap

**Start the Automatic Set Up for the New iPhone**

1. **Positioning**
   ➢ Place both old and new iPhone beside each other on a table.
2. **Old iPhone**
   ➢ Unlock the old iPhone and let it be on Homescreen.
3. **New iPhone**
   ➢ Press the switch button to "On" the new iPhone.
   ➢ Swipe up Hello, within a second your new iPhone will be seen on the screen of the old iPhone.
4. **Set Up New iPhone (Old iPhone)**
   ➢ Under the new iPhone's image hit the **Continue** bar.
   ➢ Within a second a round white shape Camera space will show up for you to capture the moving circular eruption on the new iPhone.
   ➢ Take the old iPhone above the new iPhone, let the rear Camera focus on the moving circular eruption, to be viewed in the center of the round Viewfinder space on the old iPhone above.
   ➢ Hold on till you will see "**Finish on New iPhone**" on the old iPhone before you will return it to its formal position.

44

While the old iPhone is transferring the information into the new iPhone then go to the **new iPhone** to continue.

5. Enter Passcode of Old iPhone **(New iPhone)**
   ➢ Type the Passcode of your old iPhone without making a mistake. Setting Up Your iPhone will show on the screen. Wait till you will see Face ID.
6. Face ID
   ➢ Hit on the **Continue** bar.
   ➢ Hit on "**Get Started**" bar
   ➢ Focus your eyes on the Front-Facing Camera Sensor and let your head be in the middle of the round Viewfinder frame on the screen.
   ➢ As you are turning your head gradually the surrounding lines of the round frame will be changing to green, keep turning your head and let every side of your head be captured by the Camera sensor till the surrounding lines are completely changed to green.
   ➢ If the first Face ID scanner is successful, hit on **Continue** bar and move your head in either the same or opposite way, once the second Face ID scanner is complete another page will show and tell you that "**Face ID is Now Set-Up**"

Old iPhone | New iPhone
Step 11
Step 12
Step 13
Step 14
Step 15
Step 16
Key: Where to Tap ✓

45

➢ Hit on **Continue** bar

7. Face ID (If you do not want Face ID for now)

➢ For "later Face ID Settings" hit the second option **Set Up Later in Settings.**

8. Transfer Your Data

➢ Tap on **Transfer from iPhone.** If you have updated all your apps and data, you are good to go.

➢ You may also choose **Transfer from iCloud** if you are very sure that it is up to date. You may tap on **Other Options** to select any other device like Android, Mac, PC, etc.

9. Terms and Condition

Read and digest the terms and conditions for you to know how you could successfully use your iPhone and follow them strictly. Tap on the **Agree** option at the bottom right of the screen.

10. Settings From Other iPhone

➢ Hit on the **Continue** bar to proceed.

11. Keep Your iPhone Up to Date

➢ Choose the below option of **Install Update Manually.**

12. Apple Pay

Enter your Apple Wallet detail if it is available with you by hitting on **Continue** bar.

But, choose the "**Set Up Later in Wallet**" option below if you don't have.

13. Apple Watch

Old iPhone | New iPhone

Step 16b

Step 16c

Step 16d

Leave Them for Some Hours to Completely Move All The Apps and Activate The New iPhone to Make Use of All The Latest Apps

46

➢ Tap on **Set Up Later** under the continue bar to proceed.

**14.** Apple Analytics
Select the **Don't Share** option below Share with App Developers. The next interface will show you how the data is moving from your old iPhone to the new iPhone.

**15.** Old iPhone

When all the data are completely moved into your new iPhone XS or XS Max, it will show on the screen of the old iPhone that "**Transfer Complete**".

Hit on **Continue** bar to enter the Homescreen of your old iPhone.

**16.** New iPhone

The New iPhone will show Apple's image on the screen. After a while, it will change the screen face to a white interface. Swipe Up the screen from the bottom center and launch into the data loading with the Apple image interface on the new iPhone XS or XS Max.

You have to endure enough to allow all the data and apps to absolutely moving from old iPhone to new iPhone because the uncompleted Apps will appear black with a faded icon image on the Homescreen. You will only see the icons that are completely loaded on your screen as they have appeared on your old iPhone.

# How Android User Could Transfer Data and Vital Documents into iPhone XS or XS Max

As a beginner that is very new to the use of the iPhone, you need to upgrade all your previous data and apps on your Android phone.

✓ You should also make sure that your Android Phone Battery and iPhone Battery are 100% charged.
✓ Use a strong Wi-Fi Network and turn On your Bluetooth. Alternatively, you can initially do the **manual setup** of the new iPhone for you to use the new iPhone Hotspot Wi-Fi

Connection on your Android to fast track the data or document transfer.

## Take these steps on your old Android Phone

Homescreen

> Hit on Google Play Icon.

Google Play

> Hit on the text field of Google Play at the top of the page
> Use Keyboard to enter **Move to iOS** and tap on the suggested **Move to iOS** keyword dropdown.

Move to 1OS

Hit on **Open** bar

> Do not hit on **Continue** until you are on the page of Apps & Data where you will first hit on **Move Data from Android**

## On your iPhone XS or XS Max

1. Click the **Power button** on the right side of the iPhone XS or XS Max.
2. Swipe Up the **Hello** page from the bottom and select your **language** (e.g. English).

Select Your Country or Region

1. Scroll down to select your Country by tapping on it.

**2.** Allow it to complete the **Setting Language...** processing.

**Quick Start:** Hit on **Set Up Manually.**

**Choose a Wi-Fi Network:** Select the exact **Wi-Fi network** you are using.

**Enter Password:**

1. Type the **"Password" for the Wi-Fi** correctly into the **Password Text Field.**
2. Hit on **Join** at the top right of the page.

**Data and Privacy:** Hit on **Continue Bar**

**Face ID:** Hit on **Set Up Later in Settings.** If you have not done the Face ID.

**Create Passcode:**

1. Hit on **Passcode Options** and select on a dialog box **Don't Use Passcode.** It is optional, you may create the Passcode if you want to.
2. On another dialog box showing that "**Using a Passcode is Highly Recommended**"

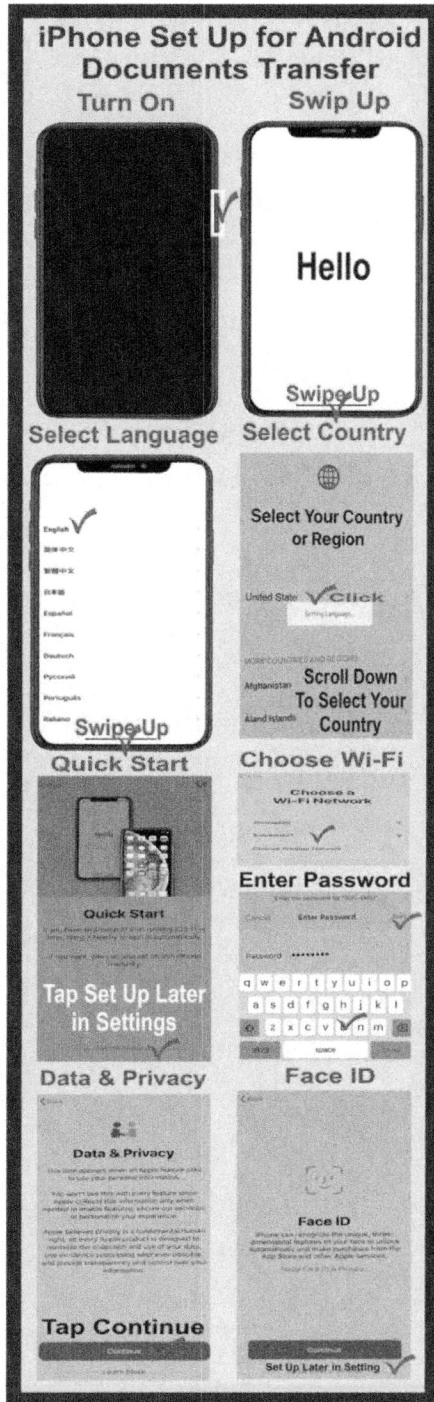

49

select "**Don't Use Passcode**" again to continue.

**Apps & Data:** Hit on **Move Data from Android.**

➡ iOS Move from Android

> ➤ Hit on **Continue** below
> ➤ Type the "**Code**" that shows on the screen of your iPhone into your Android phone.

**On Android Phone**

Move to iOS

> ➤ Hit on **Continue** above the iOS phone image.

Terms and Conditions

> ➤ Hit on **Agree**

Find Your Code

> ➤ Hit on **Next** at the top angle of the screen.

Enter Code

> ➤ Use the Keypad to enter the **Code** on the iPhone into your Android Phone.

Transfer Data:

> ➤ Select all the documents or data that you wanted to send from your Android to your new iPhone.

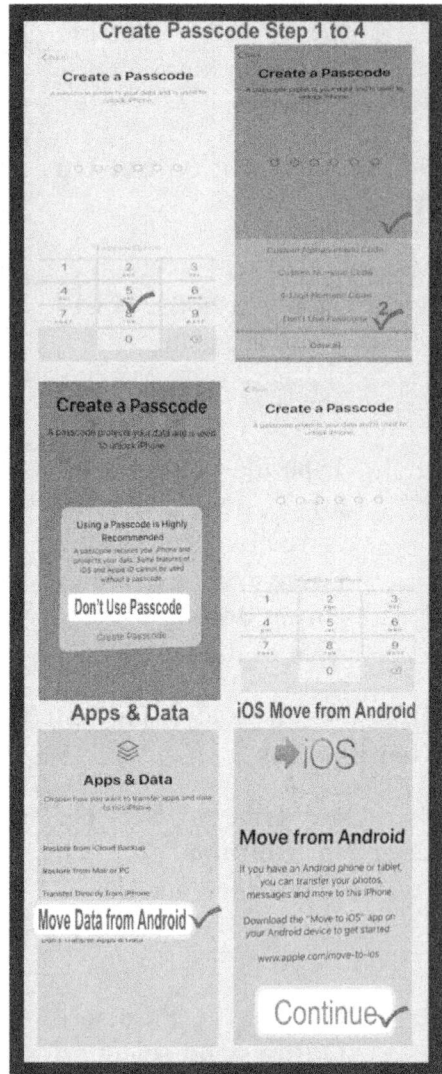

➤ Hit on **Next** at the top corner of the screen.

If you do not tap on **Next** at the top right of the Android phone your iPhone will keep waiting for you to complete the command.

Hint: Do not switch to other apps or turn off the android phone until the transfer is complete.

Ensure you position your Android phone very close to your iPhone.

If you have taken too much time before you enter the code into your Android Phone the transfer may be impossible.

If you experienced unsuccessful transfer, immediately, hit **Back** at the top left of the iPhone screen and re-tap on **Continue** to get another code. Enter the code fast into your Android Phone.

As soon as the transfer is complete on your new iPhone then tap on **Continue Setting Up iPhone.**

**Continue your iPhone setup steps from Step 13 above under manual setup or step 9**

| Android | iPhone |
|---|---|
| **Step 1** Move to iOS / Continue | ◆iOS Move from Android **82....** Enter the 6 Numbers on your Android Phone |
| **Step 2** Terms & Conditions / Disagree / Agree | |
| **Step 3** Next / Find Your Code | |
| **Step 4** Enter Code **82....** | |
| **Step 5** Move to iOS / Connecting to iPhone... | Allow it to Connect |
| **Step 6** Next / Transfer Data / Choose what you would like to move to your iPhone / Google Account / Photo | **Step 6** ➡iOS / Move from Android / Waiting for "My Android"... / On your Android device, choose what you would like to copy to your iPhone |
| **Step 7** Move to iOS / Transferring... 21% / Do not switch to other apps or turn off this device until the transfer is complete | **Step 7** ➡iOS / Move from Android / Transferring from "My Android" / Time remaining: 3 minute |
| **Step 8** Transfer Complete / Done / Recycle your Android Phone | **Step 8** ➡iOS / Transfer Complete / Continue Setting Up iPhone |

under automatic setup to complete the iPhone setup.

# GUIDE THREE

## How You Can Use Default & Customized Controls On iPhone XS & XS Max

Control Center is a slide page that contains all the basic application icons (symbols) that you can quickly get to on either iPhone Lock-Screen or Homescreen.

There are lots of apps with their operational icons on your iPhone Settings that can be customized to be in the Control Center for you to quickly reach.

Basically, by default the following apps and operational icons are in your Control Center:

- ✓ Airplane Mode
- ✓ Cellular Service
- ✓ Wi-Fi Network
- ✓ Bluetooth
- ✓ Music Panel
- ✓ Screen Lock Rotation Icon
- ✓ Do Not Disturb
- ✓ Screen Mirroring Icon
- ✓ Screen Light Control (Contains True Tone & Night Shift)
- ✓ Volume Control
- ✓ Flash
- ✓ Timer
- ✓ Calculator
- ✓ Camera

**Airplane Mode Icon:** It is used to keep your iPhone out of cellular service or network activity when you are on the Airplane board. It is activated when you hit on the icon surface.

**Cellular Service Icon:** It is used to activate the cellular service network provided by your SIM cellular

53

provider. Hit on the surface of the icon to see the name of the network provider and active bar at the top right of your iPhone.

**Wi-Fi Network Icon:** This is a data-using network that could be activated through **Personal Hotspot** in the Settings or received from an external device like iPhone, Android, Mac, iPad, or PC hotspot via Wi-Fi connectivity.

**Bluetooth Icon:** This is used to receive or transfer any app data or document from, or to other Bluetooth supporting devices. Hit the surface of the icon to activate the features. You can use it to send sound from your iPhone to another **Bluetooth** supporting sound device to play the sound aloud. You can send one document at a time.

**Music Panel**: You can use this to play and regulate the sound volume of music from your *YouTube* or iPhone music sound. Hit on the surface of the *Play Panel* to control the sound.

**Screen Lock Rotation:** This will prevent your iPhone screen display to instantly move from portrait to landscape at any quick repositioning of the iPhone to the landscape. Hit the icon to permanent the portrait screen display but if you want to use your iPhone to watch the **video** you can re-tap the icon to deactivate the effect.

**Do Not Disturb:** You can use it to stop your iPhone from ringing, vibrating, or notifying you when you are in an important gathering, meeting, on the Airplane board, or driving a car.

**Screen Mirroring Icon**: This will enable you to see what is on the screen of your iPhone on your Mac, PC, Projector, or TV through the use of a specific cable connector. Hit the surface of the icon to set the device connection and activate the application.

**Screen Light Control:** It is used to control the brightness and dimness of the screen light. If you want the screen light to be brighter, put your finger on the bright region of the control and move your finger up. But, if you want the screen face to look dim or dark move your finger from up to down.

When you press down the control **Night Shift** and **True Tone** will appear below the screen.

You can further change the mode to **Night Shift** mode that will change the screen appearance to yellowish-cream like the evening period to protect your sight (eyes).

Although by default (i.e. from the factory) it is set to **True Tone**, the icon activation appears blue.

**Volume Control:** It is used to control ring tone, alarm, video, or audio sound volume on your iPhone. Place your finger on the surface of the volume icon and high the volume by moving up your finger or low the volume by moving down your finger.

**Flash Icon:** It is used to "On" **Touch/Flashlight** at the back of your iPhone. If you hit the **Flash icon** once immediately the Flashlight will display for you to see clearly or to make the back environment of your iPhone look like daylight and helps quick search.

**Timer Icon:** It is used to set various **Timer** formats and display the Timer on the **Homescreen.** Once you hit on the **Timer** icon you will access every detail of **Timer Setting.**

**Calculator Icon**: It is used for adding, dividing, subtracting, and multiplying numbers in mathematical calculations by mathematician, accountant, statistician, or everyone, and it can be extensively changed to a scientific calculator for a scientist to calculate advance calculation that involves cosine, sine, tangent, etc. Hit the **Calculator** icon for it to appear.

**Camera Icon:** It is quickly used to access a **Camera** page for you to take pictures and make videos. Tap on the Camera icon to get into the page instantly.

# *How You Can Add More of Apps' Controls in Control Center*

**Customize Apps into Control Center**

**Homescreen:** Hit on **Settings Icon.**

**Settings:** Move down the page and hit on **Control Center**.

**Control Center**

> ➢ Hit on **Customize Control**.
> ➢ You will see **Access Within Apps**, put the activation button On if not activated by hitting on the activator.
> ➢ Hit on **Customize Control**.

**Customize Control**

> ➢ You will first see those controls that are in the Control Center listed above with a red circle having minus (remove) at the center that can be used to remove any of the controls from the Control Center if you deliberately hit on it.
> ➢ More listed Controls below are the available controls that you can add to those apps controls in the control center when you hit on the green circle having a cross sign (add) at the center. These are some of the controls you can add with those I have previously mentioned above:

Accessibility Shortcut, Apple TV Remote

Alarm,  Magnifier,  Text Size,  Note,  Guide Access,  Do Not Disturb While Driving,  Low Power Mode,  Voice Mail,  Stopwatch... and many others.

➢ Keep tapping on the **Back** icon at the top-left region of the iPhone to return to Homescreen or **Swipe Up** from the bottom center to return to Homescreen.

## *How You Could Create & Check Your Customized Controls from Control Center*

**View Controls on Lock Screen or Homescreen**

➢ Place your finger at the top right side of your iPhone and swipe down

You will see the newly customized controls under the controls I have mentioned above.

If you do not see it, go back to Settings again to confirm if the control is still among the list of **Add More.** If you see it among the list, then hit on the **Add Circle** at the front of the control Icon to add it.

If it is not among **Add More** but among the list of those that are already in the control center then go back to the control center by swiping down the screen of the iPhone from the right side. Search carefully you will see it there.

## *How You Can Activate iPhone Screen Brightness from The Source*

Homescreen: Hit on the **Settings Icon**.

Settings: Scroll down of the page to hit on **Display & Brightness** to access the settings.

Settings: Hit on the **Brightness** activation slide to become green.

> Slide the Brightness adjuster from left to right to elevate/high the screen light or you slide the adjuster from left to right to reduce the screen light.

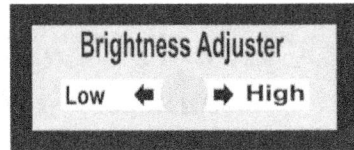

## *How Video and Music Can Be Taken from Other iPhones to Your iPhone XS & XS Max*

**Settings on your iPhone and the other iPhone**

Homescreen

> Go to **Control Center,** put On **Bluetooth** and tap the screen, or swipe up from the bottom center to go back to the Homepage.
> Hit on **Settings**

Settings: Select (tap) on **General**

General: Hit on **AirDrop**

AirDrop: Select **Everyone** and swipe up to launch the Home screen or continually tapping on the **Back icon** at the top left of the screen till you get to the Home screen.

**For iPhone Sending Video and Music** (i.e. the iPhone Sending Video and Music)

- ➢ **Videos**
  - ✓ Hit on **Photos Icon** to pick on a Video you want to select.
  - Or
- ➢ **Music**
  - ✓ Hit on **Music Icon** and select your preferred music.
- ➢ Hit on **Share Icon**
- ➢ Select **AirDrop** by tapping on it.

**On Your iPhone**

- ➢ Tap on **Accept** in the optional notification of **AirDrop.**

**On iPhone Sending Video and Music**

- ➢ Hit on your iPhone Name you are sending items to.

Instantly the new iPhone would receive the selected item.

# How You Can Use iTunes App on Your iPhone XS & XS Max

The iTunes application is an important instrument as far as adding more bits of stuff to your iPhone through your PC by sending and getting more pictures, music, video, etc. on your iPhone.

Likewise, the iTunes Store could be used to download several videos or music and play them offline on your iPhone with the use of a Wi-Fi connection. Notwithstanding, the service does not go gratis (costless), that is, you will pay for every music or audio requested at the iTunes store.

## *Syncing your iPhone with iTunes to Get Additional Benefits*

These are the following items you can add (sync) to iPhone from your iTunes library:

- ➢ Playlist,
- ➢ Movies
- ➢ Songs
- ➢ Podcasts
- ➢ Album
- ➢ Photo & Video
- ➢ Audiobooks
- ➢ Contact & Calendars

You should sync your iPhone with iTunes if you want to include the below items on your iPhone:

- ➢ **iTunes Playlists** but you will initially subscribe with **iTunes Match or Apple Music.**
- ➢ **Personal Video**
- ➢ **Calendars, Photos,** and **Contacts** provided you are not using **iCloud.**

You can also use iTunes to delete the formally added items from your iPhone.

All those lively benefits can be downloaded from the iTunes Store without you passing through the PC connection.

For you to get the iTunes Store App on your iPhone freely by using Password take the following step.

Homescreen

- ➢ Hit on **Settings Icon**

Settings: Hit on your Name or Sign In and select the **iTunes & App Store.**

iTunes & App Store: Hit on **Password Settings**

Password Settings

- ➢ Switch on Face ID for buying all you need.
- ➢ Below PURCHASE AND IN-APP PURCHASE hit on your desirable requirement (what you need).

- ➢ Below FREE DOWNLOAD you will see **Require Password**, hit the activator to become Green.
- ➢ As soon as, you are requested to provide your **Password,** then enter it.
- ➢ Hit on **OK.**

## *How You Send Audio Sound to AirPlay Speaker from Your iPhone XS & XS Max*

Homescreen: Go to **Control Center**

Control Center: Hit on **Screen Mirroring** icon

Screen Mirroring: Press the **Audio Card** down for a few seconds and the **AirPlay** icon should be tapped on.

AirPlay Speaker: Hit the **AirPlay Speaker** to be connected.

## *Why You Need App Store on Your iPhone XS & XS Max*

With the use of the Apple Store App, you can completely download many apps like WhatsApp, Facebook, iMovie, Numbers, Keynote, Pages, GarageBand… and many others through the Apple store.

Homescreen: Hit on **App Store** icon

App Store: Hit on **Continue** bar.

Browsing Page: On a request dialog box showing on your screen, tap on **Don't Allow** for Apple store not to access your location.

App Search: Look down the lower left side of the screen to hit on **Search Icon.**

- ➢ Hit the search field to type in your app request.
- ➢ As soon as you seen the App below, hit on **"Get"** at the opposite for instant **Download**.
- ➢ Make Home **Swipe Up** to see the new App Icon.

## *How You Can Easily Fix Malfunction or Freezing Problem on Your iPhone*

Unexpectedly, if your iPhone suddenly stops working or not responding to touch and the app(s) are not opening when you tap them then take the following steps to restart the iPhone.

**Stop working at any page you are on your iPhone**

**Left Side of the iPhone**

> ➢ Click **Up-Volume** button
> ➢ Click the **Down-Volume** button.

**Right Side of the iPhone**

> ➢ Use 11 seconds to press the **Power Switch** button.
> ➢ The iPhone Switch Off and reboot itself to Lock Screen.

**Lock Screen**

> ➢ Home Swipe Up.
> ➢ Provide your **Passcode**
> ➢ Home Swipe Up.

## *How You Can Fully Set Notification on Your iPhone XS or XS Max*

**Homescreen:** Hit on the **Settings** icon.

**Settings:** Move down and hit on **Notification**

**Notification:** Hit on the **App Store**

**App Store:** Give commands to your iPhone by activating the provided options that are including **Allow Notification, Badge App, Show on Lock Screen, Show in History, and Show as Banner.**

> ➢ Hit on any of these options below:
>> ✓ **Temporary Banner Show**
>> ✓ **Persistent Banner Show**

62

➢ Make Home **Swipe Up.**

**For Your iPhone Notification Preview**

It is optional for you to choose where you want the notification preview to be shown when the iPhone is locked or unlocked. After the above steps, hit on the **Back** icon for Notification at the top left of the screen to return to **Notification Page.**

**Notification**: Select **Show Preview**

**Show Preview:** You may select **Always When Unlocked or Never.** But for privacy you may tap on **When Unlocked**, that means, you can see the notification(s) only when the iPhone is unlocked.

## How to Safe the Use of Cellular Data on Your iPhone XS & XS Max

This feature will fully save your cellular data from those apps that quickly use up your cellular data through their regular automatic update on your iPhone.

**Homescreen:** Hit on the **Settings**

**Settings:** Select **Cellular**

**Cellular:** Opposite **Cellular Data** hit on **Roaming Off.**

Turn On the activation switch of **Low Data Mode** to green.

## How You Can Rescue Yourself with Emergency Free Call on Your iPhone XS & XS Max

You have to know the quick ways of activating emergency calls and the quick approach of making the call when you noticed or experienced danger around you that may result in loss of treasure or life if you do not get expert attention urgently.

**Switch Button:** Click the **Switch Button** 5 times.

Homescreen: Hit on the **Settings Icon.**

Settings: Move down to hit on **Emergency SOS**

Emergency SOS: Hit on **Also Works with 5 Clicks.**

Anytime you noticed a sudden attack or unforeseen danger, all you need to do is to click the Switch Button 5 times, and instantly you will be connected to **Emergency SOS.**

**Other Method**

Press down **Switch Button** and **Up Volume** together for the **Emergency SOS** screen to show up.

At the center of the screen, you will see **SOS Switch.** Slide the **SOS** Switch from left to right side to be connected to Emergency Call.

Hint: You can also switch off your iPhone on the same page by moving **Power Switch** from left to right.

# GUIDE FOUR

## How You Can Use All the Important Basic Futures on Your iPhone

### *How To Salience Ringtone, Vibration, or Notification Alert*

There are two major ways on your iPhone that you can use to prevent calls from ringing out or to avoid vibration or notification alert or alarm sound.

**External Buttons**

**Silent Mode Botton:** This is the first small button on the left side of the iPhone that can be moved to the front and back direction of the iPhone.

When you move the small button from the front to the backside of the iPhone you will see red on the ground of the front space and at the top of the screen notification will be shown that **Silence Mode On**. This means that you have muted the iPhone, therefore, there will be no sound from a call, alarm, and notifications but it will vibrate if you have previously activated vibration during settings.

But, when you move the button from the back to the front of the iPhone the ringtone, alarm, and notification alert sound will restore (i.e. unmute).

**Do Not Disturb**

Lock Screen or Homescreen: Swipe down the screen from the top right side of your iPhone notch.

**Do Not Disturb Icon:** Hit on the **Do Not Disturb** feature to prevent ringtone and vibration from any call, message notification, alarm, and alert sound.

**How To Make "Do Not Disturb" Work On Your iPhone**

You will have to to go to the Settings to make the feature of "Do Not Disturb" on your iPhone work by following these steps:

Homescreen: Hit on the **Settings** icon

Settings: Search down for **Do Not Disturb** and select it.

Do Not Disturb: Hit on the activation button to change to green.

**How to Set a Schedule Time for Yourself**

If you schedule the time you do not want people to disturb you with calls or messages then the first option of "Do Not Disturb" will be deactivated automatically because you cannot use both options at the same time. You have to choose one from "Do not Disturb" and "Schedule".

**Schedule:** Hit on the Schedule, to set the time you don't want people to disturb you.

**Specify Those Favorites That Your iPhone Can Allow**

You have to choose some specific favorite contacts that must be excluded from **Do Not Disturb** settings. The **Favorite Contacts** maybe your Spouse, Children, Mother, Father, and Close Relative that may seek your attention unexpectedly should in case of any unforeseen Emergency happen.

**Allow Calls From:** Hit on **Allow Call From** to select your favorites by tapping on the **Favorites** option.

**Repeated Calls**: Hit on the **Repeated Calls** Activation Switch to allow regular calls of your chosen favorites when you are busy till you pick it.

**Activate:** Hit on **Activate** to select **Manually** from the three available options which they are:

1. Automatically
2. When Connected to Car Bluetooth
3. **Manually**

Manually you will always be able to activate **Do Not Disturb** through Control Center.

**Auto-Reply To:** Select **Auto-Reply** to choose the **Favorites** and **Auto-Reply Message** that will explain why you cannot pick-up your iPhone presently.

## *Wake & Sleep Actions*

The feature will enable your iPhone sleep and wake If you are working on your iPhone and you quickly want to arrive at the **Lock Screen** without you making regular backing of pages or swiping to Homescreen.

What you will do is for you to click the **Power/Switch Button** on the right side of the iPhone. Just a click the screen will go black meaning sleep and when you make a click again on the same **Power Button** the iPhone will awake at the **Lock Screen.**

Meanwhile, any of the security authentications like Face ID or Passcode may probably require. If your Face ID failed your Passcode will be automatically displayed for you to enter.

### Auto-Sleep

Your iPhone may sleep automatically if the idle time (the time you are doing anything) has passed the time frame you set in the Settings for the iPhone screen activities, therefore, your iPhone will sleep. Wake the screen by clicking the **Switch Button** to wake it on the same page you have stopped working.

# How You Could Rearrange App's Icons on the Homescreen

Apps could be moved from one place to another place on your iPhone Home screen. You may choose to rearrange the apps in alphabetical order or base on how you will be using them regularly or how they will be more convenient for you.

**Homescreen:** For a short time press hold the screen for an optional dialog box to appear.

**Optional Dialog Box:** Hit on the **Rearrange Apps** option. Immediate the entire apps will be shaking and unstable with the *Cancel sign* attached to the left top angle of each app.

**Apps:** Place your hand on each App you wanted to move and drag the app to the favorite place. As soon as, you are through with the rearranging of the Apps as you wanted then **Swipe Up** the screen from the bottom.

## How You Can Make A File To Keep Two or More Apps On Homescreen

**Homescreen:** For a short time press the screen for a dialog box to come up.

**Dialog Box:** Hit on the **Rearrange Apps** option. Immediate the entire apps will be stirring and unstable with the *Cancel sign*

How to Rearrange
Apps on Homescreen
Step 1

Step 2

Rearrange Apps

Step 3

attached to the left top angle of each app.

Apps: Position your hand on an App and drag it on another app you want to keep in the same file. Before you release the dragged App on the below App make sure that a transparent white square shape appears around the below app. You will see the File Name text field above, hit on the text field to name the file.

If you want more than 2 Apps in a file, then continue dragging Apps on the file you have created and hit on the outer part of the file to restore and fix it.

As soon as, you are through with the rearrangement of the Apps as you wanted then **Swipe Up** the screen from the bottom, the whole apps will come back to normal.

**How To Bring Out Those Apps From The Created Files**

Created File

> **Two Apps in a File**, hold-down the file for a dialog box to show up for you to tap on **Rearrange Apps.** Immediately, the two Apps will be released from the file and show as an individual app on the Homescreen.
> **More than Two Apps in a File,** hold-down the file for a dialog box to show up, tap on **Rearrange Apps,** and all the Apps will be liberated.
> **If you want to be taken the Apps out of the file one after the other:**
> > ✓ Hit the file the whole Apps will be seen boldly.
> > ✓ Place your finger on any of the App and drag it out. The file will return to normal size while the removed App will also appear normal on the Home screen.
> **Swipe up** from the bottom to stabilize the apps.

# How You Can Delete Apps on the Homescreen

> ➢ Hold-down the app until you will see an optional dialog box.
> ➢ Hit on the **Delete** option. Immediately the app will be removed. *OR*
> ➢ Hold-down the app till you will see the whole app stirring and unstable with Cancel indication at the left angle the apps.
> ➢ Hit on the **Cancel sign**. Immediately the app will be removed from the page and the whole apps will automatically rearrange themselves.
> ➢ **Swipe Up** to stabilize the apps.

## How You Could Change Wallpaper of Both Lock Screen & Home Screen

Many lovely and attractive Wallpapers could be chosen to replace the default (brand wallpaper that comes with the iPhone) Wallpaper through Settings. Apple had made a provision for many options for you to select. The Wallpaper is sectioned into four categories:

Choose Wallpaper
Dynamic    Still    Live

1. Dynamic Wallpaper
2. Still Wallpaper
3. Live Wallpaper
4. Photo Wallpaper

**Dynamic Wallpaper:** The wallpaper contains several circular bubbles in different sizes that slightly increase in size on the screen.

**Still Wallpaper:** The wallpapers comprise of different designed stable images and natural picture without movement.

70

**Live Wallpaper:** The wallpaper shows movement when you touch the screen. Any image that is chosen in this category for your either Lock screen or Homescreen moves when you press down the screen. You can preview the animation before you set it for either the Lock screen or Home screen.

**Homescreen:** Hit on the **Settings** icon.

**Settings:** Scroll down of the page and select (hit/tap) **Wallpaper**

**Wallpaper:** Above the Lock Screen and Homescreen Image hit on **Choose A New Wallpaper.**

**Choose:** You will see Dynamic, Still, and Live galleries in a row with the series of your photo events arranged in the column below.

> Hit on any of the Wallpaper options provided or your customized personal photo.
> Hit on a Set option below the **Wallpaper**. But, if you do not like it, you may select **Cancel** to take you back to Wallpaper Choose page to re-choose wallpaper.
> Optional Dialog Box will display three possible options that you may separately consider. There you can choose any of these options **Set Home Screen, Set Lock Screen,** or **Set Both.**

Set Lock Screen

Set Home Screen

Set Both

Cancel

**Set Home Screen:** The Wallpaper you have chosen will only appear on Home Screen.

**Set Lock Screen:** The Wallpaper will only show on the Lock Screen.

**Set Both:** The Wallpaper will show in both the Lock Screen and Home Screen. Therefore, you can choose two different Wallpapers for the two screens (i.e. Home & Lock Screens).

# *Homescreen Precautions*

The Homescreen precautions will prevent your iPhone from performing any of these malfunctions like sudden sluggishness (moving slowly), jacking, delay or irregular response to finger touch, or auto-switch off.

1. Always ensure that all the open pages on your iPhone had been completely closed on your iPhone before you sleep the iPhone.
2. Ensure your iPhone is fully charged before you use it to browse, live chat, record longtime video or snap photo, download, upload… and many others.
3. Set *low power mode* on your iPhone to reduce the rate of energy consumption when battery capacity is 50 percent or less.
4. When the battery is low all the self-moving images (animation) like *Lock Screen Live Wallpaper* will stop working.

## How to Move from Home Screen to Lock Screen

Homescreen to Lock Screen: Swipe down the left side of the Notch of your iPhone, alternatively place a finger at the center of the Notch bottom frame, and swipe down the screen toward the bottom of the iPhone. The Lock Screen will show.

## How to Reduce Open Pages into the App icons on the Homescreen

Homescreen

- ➢ Hit on two-three different apps' icons on the Homescreen.
- ➢ Place your finger at the bottom center of the screen of the page.
- ➢ Slightly move up your finger for a small distance and take off your finger from the screen. You will see the app's page entering the app icon on the Homescreen.

## How to See the Reduced or Minimized Apps' Pages

### Homescreen (Middle Screen Expose)

> ➢ Move up your finger from the bottom center of the iPhone screen and slightly move it in an inverted seven Γ direction.
> ➢ As your finger is moving toward the right side of the iPhone you will see those open pages coming out from the left side of the screen.
> ➢ You can hit on any of the reduced opened app pages you still want to revisit to work on or get more information from.

### Homescreen (Bottom Screen Expose)

> ➢ Place your finger on the first end of the horizontal Homescreen Bar at the bottom center of the iPhone and move your finger to the second end of the parallel bar.
> ➢ As you are moving the finger the page will be coming out one after the other. You can move from right to left or vice versa.
> ➢ Hit on any page you are looking for and it will fully display on the screen of the iPhone.

## How to Completely Delete the Reduced Apps' Pages

### Page Pressing Down Method (after the exposed steps)

> ➢ When you press down the minimized apps you have opened one by one for a while, they will show a **Remove Sign** (a red circle containing minus inside) at the left top edge of their pages.
> ➢ Hit the **Remove** sign to completely delete the minimized page(s).

### Swiping Method (after the exposed steps)

> ➢ Place a finger on the individual reduced open app and swipe up further to completely remove the page from the iPhone.

The complete removal of the reduced opened pages on your iPhone regularly will prevent your iPhone from an abnormal slowdown of the iPhone speed efficiency.

## *How You Can Ensure Low Power Mode Battery Manager*

The use of battery mode on your iPhone will enable you to use your averagely charged battery three times longer than usual battery strength.

When you have set the battery mode on your iPhone to be active at a 50% charged level of the battery, it will actively reduce many apps that are internally using the battery abnormally. However, the brightness of the screen light will be regulated according to the level of brightness you have set for **Low Power Mode** in the settings.

The Live Wallpaper will stop working when battery mode is active.

### Activate Through Settings

Homescreen: Hit on the **Settings Icon.**

Settings: Move down the page to hit on **Battery**

Battery:

- ➤ Hit on the **Low Power Mode** to be activated by changing the button to Green.
- ➤ Go back to the Home screen by backing the pages or swiping up from the bottom center of the iPhone.

### Activate Through Control Center

You can quickly activate the **Low Power Mode** Manually if you have customized the control through settings. If you want to know how to customize control, go to Guide Three and read how to **add more of the apps' controls in the Control center**.

**Homescreen/Lock Screen:** Place your hand at the right side of the Notch above and swipe down to launch **Control Center.**

**Control Center:** Hit on **Low Power Mode** icon to activate the feature on the iPhone. The icon surrounding will change to white and the battery charge level will be yellow if it is activated.

## *How You Can Improve Battery Life-Time Through Auto-Lock Control*

Auto-lock comes to action immediately the idle time interval you have set has elapsed. That is, the iPhone will automatically lock itself after the seconds or minutes you have given to your iPhone to be active when you have stopped using it has passed.

In the Settings, you can instruct your iPhone to lock itself at any of this period below or you may even choose "Never" which is not helpful to the iPhone Battery.

➢ 30 Seconds
➢ 1–5 Minutes

**Homescreen:** Hit on **Settings Icon.**

**Settings:** Gently move down of the page to select on **Display & Brightness.**

Display & Brightness

➢ Hit on the **Brightness** activating switch to become Green.
➢ As you have activated the switch the Brightness regulator will be active. Then Move the Brightness regulator toward the left to reduce the light intensity.

**Night Shift:** If you have not activated the **Night Shift** hit on it and put it "ON". After you have activated it, go to the Control center to deactivate it by pressing down the **Screen Light Control** (Brightness control) and hit on **True Tone.**

**Auto-Lock:** Hit on the Auto-Lock to select your preferred time that you want your iPhone to remain active when you are doing anything.

**Rise to Wake:** Put "On" the activator, so that you may hit your iPhone screen when it is about to sleep.

**Text Size:** If you are not satisfied with the font size of the whole text on your iPhone you can go ahead and hit the **Text Size.** Move the Knob regulator toward the right to enlarge the text size on your iPhone screen. But, If, it is already too large, you can then move the knob regulator toward the left. (Optional)

**Bold Text:** You can make all the text on your iPhone screen to appear bold if you are not satisfied with the current look of the text font on your iPhone.

Hint: If you alter the text size or bold text, it will surely affect all the words on your iPhone.

# GUIDE FIVE

## How You Can Create Security IDs on Your iPhone XS & XS Max

### *How to Get a Secure Apple ID on Your iPhone*

Your iPhone and Apple Pay Credit Card safety are 100% guaranteed with the use of App Identity (ID). Apple Pay Credit Card will enable you to buy more applications on your iPhone, create more lively activities, activation, or settings of different apps… and many others.

You need to have one iPhone ID to link all your Apple devices like Apple iPhones, iPods, Macbook, iMac, Mac, and Watch together. That is if you are privileged to have more than one same or different types of Apple's devices.

**How To Create Your Apple ID Process**

1.  Homescreen Approach the Settings Icon by hitting on it.
2.  Settings: Look at the side of Profile Picture at the top and hit on **Sign In to Your iPhone.**
3.  Apple ID
    - In the Email text field, type your active **Email Address**.
    - Look at the top right angle of the screen to tap on **Next.**
    - Hit on an option of Don't Have An Apple ID
    - You will see an informative box with **Create Apple ID.** Tap on the option.
4.  Date of Birth
    - Type in your **Date of Birth** in the provided text field.
    - At the top angle of the screen hit on **Next.**
5.  Name: Provide your **Name and Last Name** into the text field and hit on **Next.**
6.  Email

- ➤ Make sure you enter the initial **Email** without typographical mistake or choose to **Get Free iCloud Email Address** and hit on the **Next** option.
- ➤ If you choose **Free iCloud Email** tap on **Next** and **Continue.**

Password

- ➤ You will be allowed two times to type your **Password.** Type the same password in the first password text field into the second verify password text field. If incorrect it won't continue.
- ➤ Make eight and above digits of a password that can comprise of a number, uppercase, and lowercase alphabetical letters.
- ➤ Hit **Next** at the top to continue.

7. Phone Number
- ➤ Carefully choose your Country
- ➤ Type your **Phone Number** for your identity verification.

8. Verification Method: Select any of the below options:
- ➤ **Text Message**
- ➤ **Phone Call**
- ➤ Confirm your option with **Checkmark** and hit on **Next**

9. Security Questions
- ➤ Give an unforgettable answer to the security question you will be asked. You can write the question and the answer into your confidential

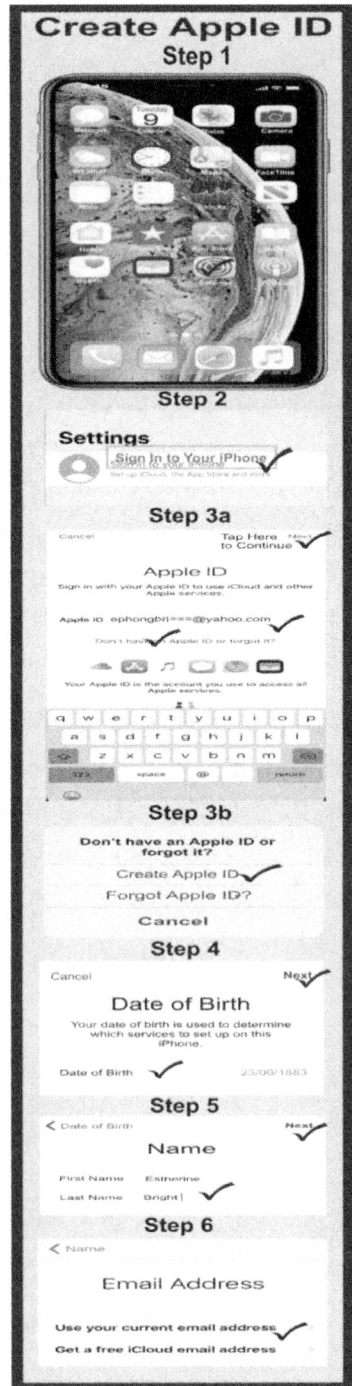

Create Apple ID
Step 1

Step 2

Settings
Sign In to Your iPhone

Step 3a

Cancel

Apple ID

Sign in with your Apple ID to use iCloud and other Apple services.

Apple ID  ephongbri===@yahoo.com

Your Apple ID is the account you use to access all Apple services.

Step 3b

Don't have an Apple ID or forgot it?

Create Apple ID
Forgot Apple ID?

Cancel

Step 4

Cancel                    Next

Date of Birth

Your date of birth is used to determine which services to set up on this iPhone.

Date of Birth          23/00/1883

Step 5

Date of Birth           Next

Name

First Name    Estherine
Last Name     Bright

Step 6

Name

Email Address

Use your current email address
Get a free iCloud email address

78

organizer/planner to subsequently guide you in giving the exact answer whenever you are asked the same question during an essential activity on your iPhone.

10. **Verification Code**
➢ Type the **Text 6-Digits Code** sent to you through your iPhone Message into the **Verification designated space** for the **Code.**

11. **Terms and Conditions**
➢ Read through the terms and conditions, digest, and get used to them or familiarize yourself with them because it is very important and hit on **Agree.** If you **Disagree,** that implies that you are not in support of Apple's Terms and Conditions guiding the Apple ID ownership as a result the Apple ID process will be discontinued /terminated.

12. **Enter iPhone Passcode:** Type your iPhone **Passcode** (4 or 6 digits). If you do not have a passcode, go to the **Add Passcode** page on the section to learn how to create your iPhone Passcode.

13. **iCloud**
➢ There will be a need for iCloud to get documents from Contact, Reminder, Notes, Calendar, and Safari on your

**Step 7**

< Email                    Next

**Password**

Password  •••••••••
Verify    •••••••••

**Step 8**
**3 Security Questions**
**Step 9**
**Phone Number**

Enter a phone number that can be used to verify your identity when you sign in on a new device or if you have forgotten your password

Country    +1 (United State)
Number     Enter Your Number

**Step 10**

< Back                     Next

**Verification Code**

Enter the verification code to

— — — — — —

**Step 11**

**Terms and Conditions**

Send by Email

**IMPORTANT**
Please read the following terms before using your iOS device. By using your iOS device, you are agreeing to be bound by the iOS Terms and Conditions. If you choose to use iCloud or Game Center, or both, you are agreeing to be bound by the respective iCloud and Game Center Terms and Conditions.

A. iOS Terms and Conditions
B. iCloud Terms and Conditions
C. Game Center Terms and Conditions
D. Privacy Policy

Scroll Down to Read More
Disagree                    Agree

**Step 12**

**Enter iPhone Passcode**

The passcode you use to unlock this iPhone will be used to confirm your identity when signing into iCloud on a new device

● ● ● ● ● ●

**Step 13**

What would you like to do with existing local Safari data on you iPhone?

Merge

iPhone. Therefore, hit on the **Merge** option.

> You may consider the other option of **Don't Merge** if you are having any otherwise opinion on their synchronization.

**14.**

> On the box accept by tapping on **OK.**

**Hint:** You will see your Full Name appear where you saw Sign in to Your iPhone. Anytime you want to sign in to your iPhone hit on your Name and continue.

Now, you have created an Apple ID for yourself. Please you need to keep email & password details carefully to prevent false operators or fraudsters using your iPhone for illegal activities.

**How To Change Your Apple ID Process**

Homescreen: Approach the Settings Icon by hitting on it.

Settings: Look at the Profile Name beside Profile Picture at the top hit on **Name.**

Password & Security

> Hit on **Change Password**
> Type in your valid **Password.**
> Type in your **New Password**
> Type in your **New Password** again for confirmation
> Hit on **Change Password**

**How To Sign In Apple ID On Your iPhone Process**

Homescreen: Approach the Settings Icon by hitting on it.

Settings: Look at the Profile Name beside Profile Picture at the top hit on **Sign In to Your iPhone.**

Apple ID

> In the Email text field, type your active **Email Address**.
> Look at the top right angle of the screen to hit on **Next.**

80

In the Password text field type in complex and easy to remember **Password**. Better still write it you're your confidential organizer.

➢ Look at the top right angle of the screen to tap on **Next.**
➢ In the last part of the page, you will see Sign Out and hit on it to leave the page.

Now, you have added your Apple ID on your iPhone.

**How To Recover Your Forgot Apple ID Process**

Homescreen: Approach the **Settings Icon** by hitting on it.

Settings: Look at the Profile Name beside Profile Picture at the top hit on **Sign In to Your iPhone.**

Apple ID:

➢ First and foremost, type your correct Email add into the email text field.
➢ Look below you will see a 2-in-1 question state thus, Don't have an Apple ID or Forgot it?
➢ Hit on **Forgot it.**
➢ **On Informative Box** hit on **Forgot Apple ID.**
➢ Firstly, you will type in a new **Password** and secondly type

**Sign In Apple ID**
Step 1

Step 2

**Settings**
Sign In to Your iPhone
Set up iCloud, the App Store and more

Step 3a

Cancel          Tap Here   Next
               to Continue  3

Apple ID

Sign in with your Apple ID to use iCloud and other Apple services.

Apple ID   ephongbri===@yahoo.com   2

Don't have an Apple ID or forgot it?

Your Apple ID is the account you use to access all Apple services.

q w e r t y u i o p
a s d f g h j k l
z x c v b n m
123   space   @   return

Step 3b

Cancel                        Next  2

Apple ID

Sign in with your Apple ID to use iCloud and other Apple services.

Apple ID   ephongbri===@yahoo.com
Password   ••••••••••   1

Step 3c

< Settings      Apple ID

EB

**Ephong Bright**

Name, Phone Numbers, Email
Password & Security
Payment & Shipping              None >
Subscriptions

iCloud
iTunes & App Store
Find My
Family Sharing

iPhone

Sign Out

the same password for the system to verify the correctness.

➤ Go to the top right angle of the screen to tap on **Next.**

You can verify it by tapping on Sign In, Type your submitted email, tap next, type your new approved Password, and tap next.

## *How You Can Correctly Do Your Face ID*

Face ID is a strong security tool that you can use to prevent fake users from using your iPhone. The use of Face ID on your iPhone will strongly enhance your iPhone security. It can be used to Unlock your iPhone.

You can use Face ID to buy things from iTunes Store, Apple Store, Apple Book with the use of your Apple pay.

Face ID in these modern developed iPhones X has replaced Touch ID in the lower iPhones, as a result, you will see Face ID & Passcode together under Settings on your new iPhone not Touch ID & Passcode.

But, it is less effective among the identical twins that are physically looking alike. It will be difficult for your iPhone Face ID infrared sensor to identify or differentiate the facially identical people.

**How You Can Create Face ID via Settings Process**

Homescreen: Approach the **Settings Icon** by hitting on it.

Settings: Search down to hit on **Set Up Face ID.**

Camera

➤ The Camera should be positioned in a portrait to capture your face. Don't allow any other person to stay behind you when you are taking your face.

➤ Hit on the "**Get Started**" bar.

➤ Let your face be boldly covered in the Camera view center.

➤ Focus your eyes on the Front-Facing Camera Sensor and let your head be in the middle of the round frame on the screen.

➢ As you are turning your head gradually the surrounding lines of the round frame will be changing to green, keep turning your head and let every side of your head be captured by the Camera sensor till the surrounding lines are completely changed to green.

➢ If the first Face ID scanner is successful, hit on the **Continue** bar and turn your head in either the same or opposite way again, once the second Face ID scanner is complete, hit on **Done** bar.

Hint: If you are unable to turn your head or stiff neck, hit on **Accessibility.**

## *How to Create an Unbreakable & Safe Passcode*

Most of the time your iPhone will always ask you to create a personal Passcode to alternate Face ID to unlock your iPhone. In a situation that you are having an identical twin-face that the Face ID may compromise, you should have a Passcode that is only known to you, then you can use the Passcode to prevent your twin from accessing your iPhone without your consent.

In a situation whereby the Face ID failed to identify your face because of the face transformation you applied (i.e. face mask, excessive face makeup, etc.) then automatically your iPhone will request for your iPhone instead.

Surely, your iPhone will ask for Passcode anytime you perform the below tasks on your iPhone:

➢ For Installation of iOS
➢ Restarting or Switching On of Your iPhone.
➢ To Remove/Delete All The Data on Your iPhone.
➢ To Change or Access Passcode Settings on Your iPhone.
➢ To Perform Software Update.

**How You Can Create Passcode via Settings Process**

**Homescreen:** Approach the **Settings Icon** by hitting on it.

**Settings:** Search down the page and select the **Face ID & Passcode** option.

**Face ID & Passcode**

> ➤ Search down the page hit on **Turn Passcode On** option.
> ➤ By default, you will see 6 digits passcode which you can change to a 4-digits passcode.
> ➤ But, if you are comfortable with the 6-digits type, then input complex **Passcode** that will have the mixture of Number, Small Case, and Capital Case of Alphabets.
> ➤ For 4-digits Passcode, hit on **Passcode Options** above the Keyboard and tap on the third option.
>> ✓ A Custom Alphanumeric Code
>> ✓ A Custom Numeric Code
>> ✓ **4-Digit Numeric Code**
> ➤ Re-type the complex Passcode for confirmation

Hint: You have to make your Passcode to be complex to prevent passcode hackers or guessers from predicting your passcode. Therefore, mix the passcode digits by selecting **Alphanumeric Code** and write it on your planner for record purposes.

***Have you suspected that you present Passcode has been exposed to the wrong person?***

***Are you noticing suspicious operations on your iPhone?***

Then, take a protective wise approach by changing the present passcode to a new Passcode.

**How To Change Exposed Present Passcode Process**

**Homescreen:** Hit on **Settings Icon**.

**Settings:** Search down the page and select the **Face ID & Passcode** option.

**Face ID & Passcode:** Search down the page and hit on **Change Passcode** option.

**Change Passcode:**

> ➢ If you are using 6 or 4-Digits Password, type the insecure Password.
> ➢ The New Passcode will be requested to be re-typed twice.

Once you type the last digit, it will automatically approve and move to the previous page.

## *Activation of Apps in iCloud Account*

The activation of apps in the iCloud account will determine the number of apps data that will be automatically uploaded and stored in iCloud storage for you to access them from all your devices. There are lots of suggested apps on your iPhone you can backup and store in the iCloud storage.

This can only be done if you switch on those apps on the iCloud page. Follow the below steps to select the appropriate apps that you want to back up with iCloud.

Therefore, you have to make more storage space available on your iPhone.

The example of the Apps is *Photo, Mail, Contacts, Calendars, Reminders, Notes, Messages, Safari, News, Stocks, Home, Health, Wallet, Game Center, and Siri.*

**Homescreen:** Approach the **Settings Icon** by hitting on it.

**Settings:** Look at the Profile Name beside Profile Picture at the top hit on **Sign In to Your iPhone.**

**Apple ID:** Look at the middle of the page and hit on the **iCloud** option.

**iCloud:** Hit the apps activation switch to change the switch look to green appearance.

**Keychain:**

> ➢ Hit on **Keychain** to turn "On" the **iCloud Keychain** switch.
> ➢ Return to the iCloud page by tapping on the **Back Arrow of iCloud** at the top left angle of the screen.

Hint: In all the devices you are using, it will constantly retain the credit card details and password you have accepted.

**Find My iPhone**

> ➢ Select **Find My iPhone** below the Keychain option under iCloud.
> ➢ Hit on **Find My iPhone** switch to activate it.
> ➢ Return to the iCloud page by tapping on the **Back Arrow of iCloud** at the top left angle of the screen.

Hint: This will enable you to locate, lock, activate, or erase your iPhone and other approved equipment if you produce your **Password**.

**iCloud Backup**

> ➢ Select **iCloud Backup** option
> ➢ Hit on **iCloud Backup** to activate the backup.
> ➢ Return to the iCloud page by tapping on the **Back Arrow of iCloud** at the top left angle of the screen.

**iCloud Drive:** It will accept all apps to store data and documents in iCloud.

> ➢ Hit on **iCloud Drive** to activate it.
> ➢ Move to the top left of the page to tap on the **Back icon** of Apple ID.

Hit on the **Back icon** at the top of Settings and swipe up from the center bottom of the iPhone to go back to the Homescreen.

# GUIDE SIX

## All Apps You Could Use to Relate with Others on Your iPhone

Some Apps have communication features on your iPhone that could be used to express yourself with others which enable you to pass across information to people that are very important to you and also receive information from them. The Apps will give you access to hear the voice of the caller or record the conversation between both of you.

More so, through the communication app, you can make live text chat with your dearest fellows or colleagues or business partners or family, and instantly receive a reply with the use of cellular data or subscription.

Above all, you can make conference audio or video calls with numerous of people. The Apps the have the **Communication Features** are:

1. Call App
2. FaceTime App
3. Message App
4. Mail App

The Apps that help in getting more information for communication Apps are:

1. Safari App
2. Siri App
3. iTunes App

# How You Could Fully Enjoy Different Calls with Phone App on Your iPhone

The Phone app is one of the most essential primary cores of using the iPhone for communication. The use of Call App will enable you rich-out to your people of your through their phone numbers.

The people's phone number could be categorized into two places to separate the most important ones from general ones.

The most inevitable people are considered to be your **Favorites** on the iPhone while others belong to the general **Contacts.** You can assign a separate ringing tone to all contacts in **Favorites.**

By default, the Phone App is specifically positioned at the base bar of the Homescreen to ease your call making and receiving.

Source of Finding & Saving Contacts

Recents    Keypad

Favorites  |  Contacts  |  Voicemail

To save your friend contact in Phone app contacts, you will need the phone number, first and last name, email (if available), and picture (if available). But, it is very advisable to save your friend's email in the contact detail because you may need to reach him/her through your Email massage.

### Add Contact

Homescreen: Hit on the **Phone App** at the base bar of your iPhone.

### Favorites

> ➤ Hit on **Favorite** icon (Star) at the bottom left of the screen.
> ➤ Hit on **Add** icon (Cross) at the top left of your iPhone's screen.
> ➤ Go through all contact to locate the named contact or enter the name of the person into the **Search field** to quickly see the **Person's Contact.**

➢ Hit on the Contact Name

**Optional Dialog Box:** Hit on the usual way of contacting people such as Message (iMessage or Mail), Call, or FaceTime. For example, select Call.

Immediately, you will see the selected contact name among **Favorites.**

**OR**

Homescreen: Hit on the **Phone App** at the base bar of your iPhone.

Contacts

➢ Hit on **Contacts Icon** at the bottom center of the iPhone's screen.
➢ Hit on the **search field** to quickly locate the contact's name you are looking for.
➢ Hit on the contact's name to see all the person's information details, below you will see **Add to Favorites.**
➢ Hit on the Contact Name

**Optional Dialog Box:** Hit on the usual way of contacting people such as Message (iMessage or Mail), Call, or FaceTime. For example, select Call.

➢ Immediately, you will see the selected contact name among **Favorites.**

Remove a Contact from Your iPhone

You need to understand the fact that, whenever you apply to **Delete** command on any contact on your iPhone or Email account, it will completely remove it from your iPhone without a chance of retrieving/restoring it.

Therefore, you have to fully sure about the contact before you hit on **Delete** command.

Homescreen: Hit on **Contacts Icon**

89

Contacts

> Search for the **Contact's Name** through the search field
> Hit on the exact **Contacts Name**
> Hit on **Edit**
> Move down the screen to hit on **Delete Contacts.**
> For confirmation re-tap on **Delete Contacts** (Confirmatory Dialog Box). Immediately the contact will be completely removed from your iPhone Contacts' list.

**Set Sorting Order of Contacts List on Your iPhone**

The Names of everyone in your Contacts could be arranged chronological order from A-Z to ease searching of either **First or Second Name.**

You are given the privilege to instruct your iPhone on how you want the name to be arranged, that is if you want the First name to appear before the second the following setting will enable it:

Homescreen: Hit on the **Settings Icon**

Settings: Scroll down to select **Contacts**

Contacts

> **Sort Order:** This will alphabetically arrange either the First or Second Name in Contacts.
> **Display Order**: This will either display the First Name after or before Second Name.

**Short Name**: Select how the Contact's Name of yours will show in Phone, Mail, Messages, FaceTime… and other Apps.

**Move Contacts from SIM to iPhone**

You can transfer all your contacts on your SIM into your new iPhone if the SIM supports the feature it is very easy to do.

SIM Card Insertion: Insert your SIM containing the contacts you want to transfer into your iPhone.

Homescreen: Hit on the **Settings Icon**

Settings: Hit on **Contacts**

Contacts:

> ➢ Move to the middle of the screen to hit on **Import SIM Contacts.**
> ➢ Hit where the contacts should be imported from an optional dialog box that will appear.
> ➢ Hold on till the whole contacts moving process finished before you proceed.
> ➢ Access your Contact to confirm the complete importation on iPhone.

Hints: iPhone cannot save the contact(s) on SIM card, if you want to transfer contacts from iPhone to iPhone then there will be a need for you to back-up the iPhone with iCloud storage or other transferring means like PC memory, flash, etc.

### Activate and Deactivate Contacts for Mail Account

The activation of Contacts will enable you to add contacts in any of your Email Account and deactivation of Contacts will enable the removal of contact(s) from your iPhone.

Homescreen: Hit **Settings Icon**

Settings: Hit on **Password and Account**

Password and Account: Hit on the **Email Account.**

The Email Account (Gmail/Yahoo): Switch On the **Contacts Activator** to become Green.

### To Deactivate Contacts App

The Email Account (Gmail/Yahoo)

> ➢ Switch Off the **Contacts Activator** to become **White.**
> ➢ Hit **Delete from My iPhone.** Immediately the contact will be removed.

## Make Your Contacts for Email Account

**Homescreen:** Hit **Settings Icon**

**Settings:** Hit on **Password and Account**

**Password and Account:** Hit on **Add Account**

**Add Account:** Hit on your Email account and switch On **Contacts.**

If you do not have an email account you can hit on **Other** to make Contact Account such as LDAP or CardDAV account is available.

 ➢ Type your details and password.
 ➢ Hit on **Next.**

In a situation whereby you are having several accounts set up in the Contacts App and you need a particular account for the contacts:

**Homescreen:** Hit on **Contacts** App

**Contacts:** Hit **Groups** at the top left angle of the screen.


## Add New Contact to Your Default Account

This is very advisable for you if you are using more than one Email Account in your **Contacts.**

**Homescreen:** Hit on **Settings Icon**

**Settings:** Scroll down to select **Contacts**

**Contacts:** Hit on **Default Account**

**Default Account:** Select **One** of your **Email Accounts.**

92

How You Can Make A Call Conveniently

Homescreen: Hit on **Phone App**

Keypad Interface

> ➤ Type the **Contact Number** if you do not have the person's contact in your iPhone **Contact List.**
> ➤ Hit on the **Call Button.** It is the Green Circle.

End Call

> ➤ The Green Circle Button will change to Red Circle Button, it is called the **End Button.**
> ➤ Hit the **End Button** to stop the call.

Make A Call from Contacts

Keypad Interface: Look at the bottom center to hit on **Contacts.**

Contacts:

> ➤ Enter the first-two alphabetical letter that started the name of the person into the search field to speed up the quick discovery of the contact.
> ➤ Hit on the **Contact's Name**

Contact's Name: Hit on the person's Phone Number.

End Call: Hit the **End Button** to stop the call.

Add People's Phone Number to Your Contact Directly

Keypad Interface

> ➤ Dial the **Phone Number** of the person correctly.
> ➤ Hit on **Add to Contact** at the top of the screen.

**Request Dialog Box:** On a displayed **Request Dialog Box** hit **Create New Contact.**

### Create New Contact

- ➢ Type the First and Second Names
- ➢ Enter the Email of the owner of the Phone Number if you know it (optional).
- ➢ You can choose different **Ringtones** for the contact it is optional.
- ➢ Hit on **Add to Existing Contact**

### Add to Existing Contact

- ➢ Look for the **Contact**
- ➢ Enter the Number into the Number text field
- ➢ Hit on **Done.**

### Add To Contacts from Recent Called or Received Contacts

You can add the recently ended call phone number into your general Contact by following these steps on your iPhone.

**Keypad Interface:** Look below and hit **Recents** with a round clock icon.

### Recent

- ➢ You will see the recently ended phone number
- ➢ Hit on the **Info icon** in front of the phone number.

**Info:** Select **Create New Contact**

### Create New Contact

- ➢ Type the First and Second Names
- ➢ Enter the Email of the owner of the Phone Number if you know it (optional).
- ➢ You can choose different **Ringtones** for the contact it is optional.
- ➢ Hit on **Add to Existing Contact**

> ➢ Look for the **Contact**
> ➢ Enter the Number into the Number text field
> ➢ Hit on **Done.**

Now the recent call will appear with the name you used in the adding of the number into your Contacts. The person contact can be found in your overall **Contacts list** on your iPhone.

### How to Delete all Recent Contacts

A recent list comprises of the phone numbers of all those you have called, received calls and missed incoming calls, and missed outgoing calls with day and time they were called or received. You can easily remove all the recent history.

**Homescreen:** Hit on **Phone App Icon**

**Keypad Interface:** look at the bottom left of the screen and hit on **Recents** (Round Clock Icon).

Recents

> ➢ Look at the top left of the screen hit on **Clear**
> ➢ Hit on the **Clear All Recents** button showing down the screen. If you hit the **Cancel** button, it will reverse the action and the recent list will not be deleted.

## *All You Can Do When You Are on a Call*

1. *You can switch inside speaker  to outside Speaker*
2. *You can switch to Video Call.*
3. *You can allow more people to your discussion.*
4. *You can Mute the Voice.*
5. *You can Accept or Decline other incoming calls.*
6. *You can compose a message to reply to your call.*
7. *You can make use of Remind Me to program a reminder for you to return the call of the caller later.*

8. *You can search through apps (e.g. Mail, Photo, Note, Calendar, Safari, Social Media) to get relevant information. Browsing Apps will require a Wi-Fi network connection on your iPhone.*

## How to Allow or Prevent Call When You Are On A Call

**To Accept Call:** On the calling, the interface slides the Call button toward the right to answer the call.

**To Prevent the Call and Forward It into Voicemail:** Double-click the **Switch Button** at the right side of the iPhone.

**Send Message To Caller:** Hit on **Message Icon** to text messages and send them to your caller.

**Use Reminder To Recall:** You can hit on **Remind Me** to instruct reminding me to call the caller after you stop the current call.

## How You Can Make Your Voicemail Active

Voicemail has a feature that can play your recorded voice greeting to tell the reason why you are not available to receive calls at the moment and also record and play the voice of the caller that audibly delivered messages for a very short time for you to hear.

You can also choose a greeting out of some default recorded greetings for your outgoing greeting.

To make Voicemail to be active you have to go into the Setting or through Voicemail Icon in the Phone app to Set Up your **Password and Greeting**.

Homescreen: Hit on the **Phone App** icon.

Keypad Interface: below the screen hit on **Voicemail Icon** at the last bottom left.

Voicemail: Hit on **Set Up Now.**

96

> ➢ Type in the **Voicemail Password** that must be in 4-digit.
> ➢ Retype the same **Voicemail Password** to confirm your consistency.

## Greeting

> ➢ Hit on **Custom** options to make your outgoing greeting with your voice or otherwise.
> ➢ Hit on **Record** to start. (Say your greeting as you want it to be said).
> ➢ Hit on **Stop** to end the recording.
> ➢ Hit on **Play** to hear your recorded greeting.
> ➢ If you are not okay, you can re-tap the **Record.**
> ➢ If you are okay then hit on **Save**

**How to Reset Voicemail Set Up Through Settings**

**Homescreen:** Hit on the **Settings icon.**

**Settings:** Select **Phone App**

**Phone:** Hit on **Change Voicemail Password**

Password

> ➢ Hit on **New Password**
> ➢ Type in the **Previous Password**
>> ➢ Type in the **New Password**
>> ➢ Hit on **Done.**

**How to Listening to Your Voicemail**

If you are having calls that have been forwarded into Voicemail, you will see the notification number of new Voicemails at the top-right edge side of the **Voicemail Icon** at the last bottom left of the keypad interface.

Homescreen: Hit on the **Phone App** icon.

Keypad Interface: below the screen hit on **Voicemail Icon** at the last bottom left.

Voicemail

> ➢ Hit on **Message**
>
> ➢ Hit on **Play** to hear the recorded caller's voice.
> ➢ Hit on **Call Back** to replay the voice message.
> ➢ If you are satisfied with the message you can hit on Delete.

## To Call the Voicemail

Homescreen: Hit on the **Phone App** icon.

Keypad Interface: below the screen hit on **Voicemail Icon** at the last bottom left.

Voicemail:

> ➢ Hit on **Call Voicemail.**
> ➢ Hit on **End Button.**

## Send Junks and Unwanted Callers into Voicemail

This is will only allow the saved contacts on your iPhone to ring-out but unknown contacts will be sent to Voicemail

Homescreen: Hit on the **Settings icon.**

Settings: Tap on **Phone**

Phone: Hit on the **Salience Unknown Caller** activator to become Green.

## Set Call Waiting in Settings

Wi-Fi Network connection is very important to make Wi-Fi call active in Dual SIM. You will see Call Waiting when one line call is active and another incoming call occurs in another line.

Homescreen: Hit on **Settings**

Settings: Hit on **Phone App**

Phone: Select **Call Waiting** and hit on the activator to become Green.

> ➢ Make Home Swipe Up

## *How to Set Special Sound & Hepatic Rings for Calls, Messages, Alert, & Mail Notifications*

You can assign separate ringtones to different contacts in iPhone Contacts. You may consider giving similar ringtone and vibration to all the contacts in Favorite and different ringtones to some set of people in all Contacts.

You can use ringtone to know when closed family members in the Favorites are calling and when your important business partners are calling.

Homescreen: Hit on **Settings**

Settings: Hit on **Sound & Hepatics**

Sound & Hepatics

> ➢ Hit on the **Vibrate on Ring** activator to turn Green
> ➢ Hit on the **Vibrate on Silence** activator to turn Green
> ➢ Select your **Ringtone** and choose any of the default Ringtones available.

Make Special Ringtone for Individual Contact

Homescreen: Hit on **Contact App** icon

Contacts

> ➢ Search for contact through the search field.

- ➤ Hit on the **Contact**
- ➤ Hit on **Edit**
- ➤ Hit on **Ringtone**
- ➤ Select one of the **Default Ringtones**.
- ➤ Make **Home Swipe Up**.

# GUIDE SEVEN

## How You Can Fully Enjoy FaceTime App on Your iPhone XS or XS Max

FaceTime App is an interactive method of communicating with those on your iPhone Contacts.

It has a unique video communication feature that can enable you to see the face of the person you are calling or the person that called you.

Most of the time, it is important that you first and foremost send a request to the person you want to make a FaceTime video call with on either interactive iMessages interface or through an audio call that you will like to make or switch to FaceTime Video Call.

You have to ensure that the persons are using the iPhone and you are having enough Wi-Fi Data to make the call.

You can also use FaceTime to make Conference Video Call with other iPhone users in your contacts but you must notify those that will participate in the conference call on text message interface the time, the reason for the group discussion, and ask each of them if they will be available.

**Make FaceTime Set Up in Settings to be Active**

**Homescreen:** Hit on **Settings Icon**

**Settings:** Scroll down to select **FaceTime**

**FaceTime**

- ➢ Put On the **FaceTime** Activator to become Green
- ➢ Put On the **FaceTime Live Photo** Activator to become Green
- ➢ Provide your **Phone Number**
- ➢ Provide your **Apple ID**
- ➢ Provide your **Email Add** (Optional)

## Make FaceTime Audio Calls or Video Call

**Homescreen:** Hit on **FaceTime Icon**

**FaceTime:** Hit on **Add Contact** at the top right of the screen.

**Contact:** Use the search field to quickly get the contact.

**Audio Call:** Hit on the **Audio Call button** to fix the audio call.

**OR**

**Video Call:** Hit on the **Video Call button** to fix the video call.

## How to Change from Normal Audio Calls to FaceTime Video Call

On the calling interface, you will see an option of using FaceTime Video

**Video Call:** Hit on the **Video Call button** to fix a video call .

Hit on the **End button** at the lower left of the FaceTime Video call interface.

## How You Can Change from Text Message Interaction to FaceTime Call

**Homescreen:** Hit on **Messages App Icon**

**Message**

➢ Hit on the **Compose icon** at the top right of the screen.

- ➤ Type the name of the person you want to chat with into the "**To**" Search field.
- ➤ During the live iMessage chatting with your friend, hit on the name of your friend at the top center of the screen to choose FaceTime.
- ➤ Hit on **FaceTime Icon**
- ➤ Choose either **Audio or Video Call**
- ➤ Hit on End button to end the FaceTime call

## How to Make Multiple Live Chat

**Homescreen:** Hit on **Messages App Icon**

Messages

- ➤ Hit on the **Compose icon** at the top right of the screen.

- ➤ Type the **Names or Phone Number or Email Add** of all persons you want to chat with into the "**To**" Search field. For example, *Hannah Berm, Daniel Rose, Dan Floral*
- ➤ Below the screen hit the text message field for **Keyboard** to show-up, type your text message, and hit on **Send icon** to deliver your message into the chat interface.

## How to Change the Group Conference Conversation to FaceTime Video Call

It is the same step of moving from a single chat that you will take to change your communication mode to FaceTime Video or Audio Call.

Message (Chatting Page)

- ➤ Hit on the names of your friends at the top center of the screen to choose **FaceTime**.
- ➤ Hit on **FaceTime Icon**
- ➤ Choose either **Audio or Video Call**
- ➤ Hit on End button to end the FaceTime call

How to Replace Your Face with Animoji during FaceTime Video

Homescreen: Launch **FaceTime** App

FaceTime

> On the FaceTime Call interface hit on **Video Call button.**
> Hit on **Effect Button.**
> Hit on either **Memoji** or **Animoji** available
> Scroll toward the right or left to choose.
> Hit on your preferred Memoji or Animoji. Immediately your face will be replaced with chosen Memoji or Animoji.
> To remove the Memoji or Animoji hit on **Cancel** and your face reappear normally.

**If you want to change the current Memoji or Animoji:** Restart all over from the beginning of the above process and reselect the new Memoji of Animoji of your choice.

## *Other Ways of Using Message App on Your iPhone*

You can majorly use Messages App to make a direct live chat with those who are in your iPhone contacts using iPhone through iMessage.

Also, you can use it to send a text message to those who are in your contacts using Android.

How to Compose and Reply Text Messages

Homescreen: Hit on **Messages App Icon**

Messages

> Hit on the **Compose icon** at the upper right of the screen.

> Type the name of the person you want to chat with into the "**To**" Search field.

**OR**

➤ If you want to reply to any received message in the massage App, hit on the particular message. It will launch you into the compose text message interface.
➤ Hit the text field to type your text message.
➤ Hit the **Send Button,** that is, the Blue Send Button is for iMessage ⬆ while Green Send Button is for SMS⬆.

Your iPhone will automatically determine if the text message is iMessage or SMS. Once you see the blue button showing for sending your text message that implies you are about to send iMessage to the person using iPhone but if it shows green that means, you are sending text SMS to an Android user.

**How to add Emoji to your Text Message**

Messages

➤ At the lower left side of the Keyboard hit on **Emoji** Icon
➤ You may scroll up and down or right side to select by tapping on anyone you like.
➤ Hit on the Send button to move it into the chat interface.

**How to add Effects to your Text Message**

Messages

➤ At the immediate left side of the Keyboard Text Field, you will see **App Store** Icon, hit on it
➤ Select the **Animoji icon** at the bottom roll menu 🐵 .
➤ You will see different **Animoji** images.
➤ Select Animoji you like and position it within the square view guide. Once the Animoji is registered, it will be mimicking your face and mouth movement.
➤ Hit on **Recording Button** at the bottom right side of the view frame to start recording your audio voice with Animoji. ⬤

> Hit on the same button to stop the recording and change the button to the **Send** button. It will replay itself for you to hear.

> If you are satisfied then hit on the **Send button** to forward the Animoji into the **Chat** interface for the person you are chatting with to receive and access.

> You can still reselect another Animoji below by scrolling through the arranged Animoji drawer and hit on another different Animoji to make a new recording.

> If you are not satisfied hit on the **Delete** button at the upper right.

**For Additional Effects**

> You can still go-ahead to get more Animoji in the App Store by tapping on the **App Store** icon at the lower-left corner of the screen and hit on **View Apps.**

> You can still search for "**Images**" that are very accurate to your message by tapping on **Search Icon** below.

> Hit on Find Images Field showing above the displayed images.

> Enter the types of images you are looking for like Thinking, Disagreement, Excitement, Sleeping, Busy, Hungry, Disturbed, Listening, Working… and many others. You may pick from the appearing keywords as you are entering the word.

> There is also a **Free Hand Drawing icon** that could allow you to draw anything you like and send it to the person you are chatting with.

> You can also send home videos through **YouTube, Audio Music, Recents Selfie Pictures/other Pictures, or Video** through Camera.

# How to Make Your Customized Animoji or Memoji on Your iPhone

Messages

> ➢ At the immediate left side of the Keyboard Text Field, you will see **App Store** Icon, hit on it.

> ➢ Select the **Animoji icon** at the bottom roll menu .

> ➢ Scroll toward right hit on Add/Cross Sign for **New Memoji**

> ➢ Select **Skin** and adjust it with the available set of colors and remove face spots by choosing freckles.

> ➢ Select **Hairstyle** to choose either male hairstyle or female hairstyle

> ➢ Move to **Head Shape** to select the loveliest chin.

> ➢ Move to the **Eye** section to pick the type of eye you like having on your Memoji.

> ➢ Continue to select all the parts of the face of your Memoji from the other options including **Browse, Nose & Lips, Ear** with different pretty earing, **Facial Hair** with either Mustard & Beard or Sideburns, **Eyewear** like glasses, and **Headwear** like face-caps, hat, etc., till you complete achieve a beautiful looking Memoji. It is a creative place that is full of fun.

> ➢ As soon as you are satisfied with your **Self Making Memoji** then hit on **Done** to save the Memoji and include it with the group of Animoji.

You can use your Memoji to make FaceTime video call or iMessage audio chat on the Message App interface of your iPhone.

## How to Add Animation Effect to Your Key Text Message

Messages

> ➢ Type your short text message into the text field. For example, *Stay Home Safe, Drink Responsibly, Daily Exercise Importance, Let's Jubilate, Today's Plan, etc.*

> ➢ Press down the **Send** button for a while to launch **Effect Page** contains:

- ✓ **Bubble Animation Effects:** Slam, Loud, Gentle and Invisible Ink.
- ✓ **Screen Animation Effects:** Send with Echo, Send with Confetti, Send with Spotlight… and others.

### Send with Effect

- ➤ At the upper center of the page, you will see **Bubble & Screen.**
- ➤ Hit one of the various effects menu to know the best. Once you have known the best effect, leave it on the option.
- ➤ Hit on the **Screen** option above.
- ➤ Swipe the screen from right to left to see the various screen effects. When you have seen the most suitable **Screen Effect** for your Text message then hit on the **Send** button.
- ➤ If you are not satisfied then hit on the **Cancel** button to return to the message interface.

### How to Send Voice Message

This makes the message easy to those who are not having enough time to chat or who are not very fast in a typing text message to quickly deliver their messages, as a result, they choose a short audio recording message that is précised, specific, and facts.

### Messages

- ➤ Go to the bottom left of the keyboard and hit on **Microphone Icon.**
- ➤ Start an audio message. You will see the linear sound wave of your voice as you are talking. The louder your voice the larger the width of the sound wave.
- ➤ As soon as you finished the audio message the hit **Send** button above.
- ➤ It will be seen in the chat interface.
- ➤ Look at the bottom left of the screen and hit on the Keyboard icon to return the Keyboard.

Hint: You can also dictate your message to Siri that is capable of changing all your audio dictation messages to text messages and sent it to the right contact you commanded.

## How to Fully Use Mail App to Get Good Results

Mail app is an avenue to receive and send a message(s) with the use of Electronic Mail (Email) Service Providers which include **Google** (...@gmail.com), **Yahoo** (...@ yahoo.com), **iCloud** (...@icloud.com), **Outlook.com** (...@outlook.com)... and many others.

The use of the Mail App will fully allow you to receive or send documents to loved ones and business associates. It is more officially use for a better transaction between you and other business organizations.

Mail has become the most reliable acceptable official interactive platform to provide your vital details and execution of online obligation.

Therefore, the essential processes for you to become a wonderful beneficiary user of Mail great opportunities.

There are channels through which you can get information from that can be added to your composed message such addition is called **Document Attachment.**

You can save documents with any **Microsoft Office** formats or you may directly go to a website to copy very relevant information that is helpful to clarify your message and subsequently paste it within your message.

If you already have two or more email accounts and you want to add them to your new iPhone there are some simple steps you have to do in your iPhone Settings.

To make Mail effectively functional, then you have to carry-out either manual or automatic setup in Settings on your iPhone.

## How to Put Manual Set Up for Mail App in Place

The manual is simply designed for those who are using different Emails from the suggested email accounts on the Add Account Interface. Then, the **Other** is the correct option to choose.

**Homescreen:** Hit on the **Settings** icon.

**Settings:** Move down and select **Accounts & Passwords.**

**Accounts & Passwords:** Hit on **Add Account**

**Add Account:** Look at the lower region of the screen and hit on **Other.**

**Other:** Hit on **Add Mail Account**

**New Account**

> ➤ Type your **Name**
> ➤ Type your specific **Email Account**
> ➤ Type your **Password**
> ➤ Type your **Description**
> ➤ Hit on **Next** for the setup to be finalized and the Mail will search for your Email Account.
> ➤ Once the searching is successful then hit on **Done.**

If the Email Account Settings could not be found by Mail then do the following to roundup the setup.

**Second Phase** New Account: If you

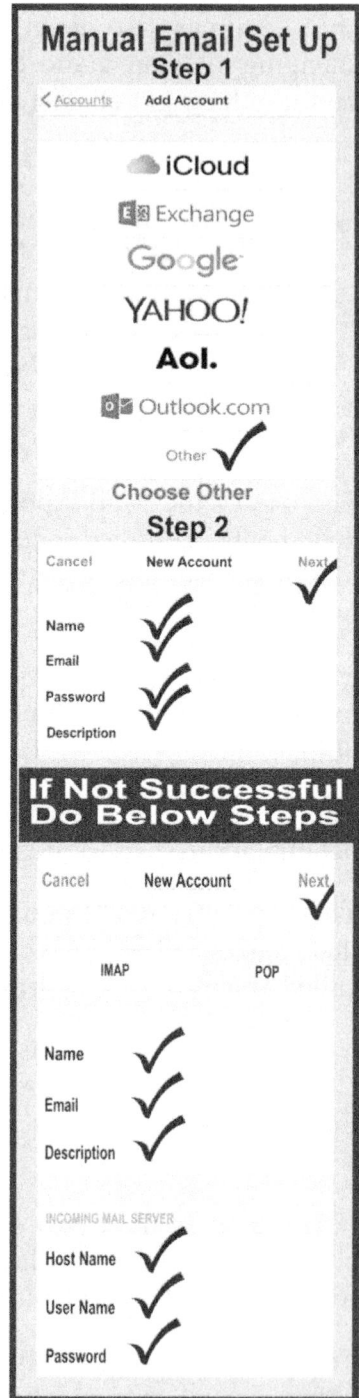

110

do not know your Email settings ask your email service provider to tell you if the email settings belong to IMAP or POP. As soon as, you confirm

- ➢ Hit on **IMAP/POP**
- ➢ Provide details on **INCOMING & OUTCOMING MAIL SERVER**
  - ✓ **Host Name**
  - ✓ **User Name** & **Password**
- ➢ Hit on **Next** at the top.
- ➢ Once your details are accurate then hit in **Save**

Your inability to provide the correct details will lead to the inability to complete the manual setup.

**How to Put Automatic Set Up for Mail App in Place**

**Homescreen:** Hit on the **Settings** icon.

**Settings:** Move down and select **Accounts & Passwords.**

**Accounts & Passwords**: Hit on **Add Account**

**Add Account:** Select your Email service source (e.g. Yahoo).

**Yahoo**

- ➢ Type your existing **Yahoo Address**
- ➢ Type correct **Password**

(If you want to look into your email account then you can hit on **Sign In**, when you are through, then **Sign Out** to return to the previous Set Up page because you still have some tasks to

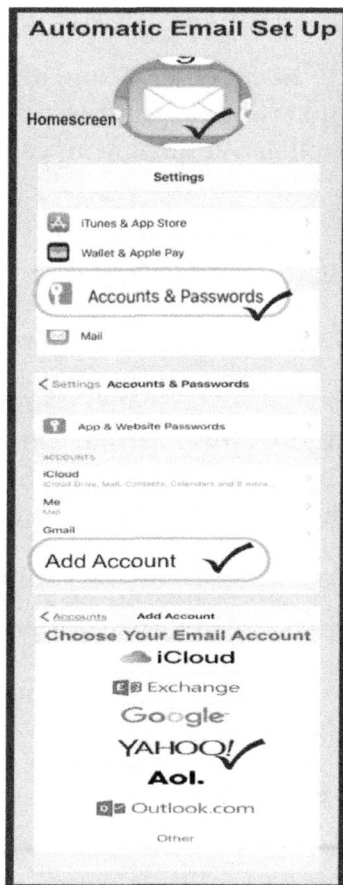

111

complete. Better still, complete the tasks before you Sign-In into your account).

> Hit on **Next** to continue and hold on for the processing to complete.

### In Your Yahoo Account (…@yahoo.com)

> Switch On the **Activator** of the following applications **Contacts App, Mail Contacts, Calendar App, Note App & Reminder App.**
> The upper right region of the screen hit on **Save.**


### How to Activate the Function of Essential Tools for Message Composition

All essential tools for a perfect write up and excellent message composition should be activated in the Settings to ensure correct spellings, arrangement, capitalization… and many others.

**Homescreen:** Hit on the **Settings icon**

**Settings:** Select **General**

**General:** Select **Keyboards**

**Keyboards:** Switch On the following **Activation buttons** of **Auto-Capitalization, Auto-Correction, Check Spelling, Enable Caps Lock, Predictive, Smart Punctuation, Character Preview, Shortcut, and Enable Dictation.**

**To Change Your Keyboard to One-Handed Keyboard**

On the same Keyboards page

**Keyboards:** Select **One-Handed Keyboard** and hit on the **Activator**

**OR**

You can also get the selection of One-Handed Keyboard directly on the Mail to compose page.

Homescreen: Hit on **Mail App**

Mail: Hit the **Compose icon** at the top right region of the screen or

select received Email and later hit on compose or reply icon.

New Message

> ➢ Hit the front of "**To:**" for text cursor to show and the Keyboard to show below.
> ➢ At the lower region of the Keyboard in the new message interface, press down the Earth icon for different types of Keyboard to show.
> ➢ Hit on either left or right-hand side Keyboard that is very convenient for you.

**How to Write and Send Email Messages**

Homescreen: First and foremost, go to the **Control Center** to put On Wi-Fi Network and hit on **Mail App**

Mail: Hit Compose Icon at the top right region of the screen or

select received Email and later hit on compose or reply icon.

New Message

> ➢ Hit the front of "**To:**" for text cursor to show and the Keyboard to show below.
> ➢ Type the **Name or Email Address** of the receiving contact (the person's or company's email address).
> ➢ Hit the front of "**Subject:**" to type a short theme of your message.

- ➢ Hit on the text field interface to start writing your text message. Once you are through then hit on the **Send icon** at the top right region of the screen ⬆.
- ➢ How to Directly Get Name or Email from Your iPhone Contact

You can directly get the name or email address of the person you want to send an email message to through the Contacts on your iPhone.

New Message: Hit on the **Add/Cross** icon to launch Contacts and use the search field to quickly locate the contact you are looking for.

### How to Attach Document to Your Message

It is advisable to attach a PDF or JPEG document to your Email because the document cannot be altered.

Mail: Hit Compose Icon at the top right region of the screen or select received Email and later hit on compose or reply icon. ✏️

New Message: After you have entered the above "**To**" info (name or email add of where you are sending a message)**, Subject and** You have composed your message.

- ➢ Press down anywhere on the message field for **Edit Menu** to show.
- ➢ Hit on the **Arrow** at the end of the **Edit menu** to select **Add Attachment.**
- ➢ It will open to your iPhone document storage and iCloud Drive. Navigate through the App you used such as **Pages App, Keynotes App...** and others.

**For Photo or Video**

➤ You can also attach pictures to your message by tapping or press down the field and be tapping on the arrow at the end till you will see **Insert Photo** or **Video.**

    ✓ It will launch out your Photo library to select your **Pictures.** Carefully navigate through the exact category you have your pictures.

    ✓ Hit on your **Pictures** and **Send** them to upload on your massage field.

## Copy Information from Website

    ✓ At the down middle of the iPhone Notch slide-down a little to see the App browsing text field.

    ✓ Enter Safari, you will see the App and hit on it to access the web page.

    ✓ Enter web add, highlight the massage, and hit copy.

    ✓ Go to the base of the horizontal bar and swipe from the left end to the right end. You will see the New Message page.

    ✓ Hit the place you want to paste the copied info to display on the message field for the edit menu to show an option of **Paste.** Hit Paste and what you copied will display.

**OR**

**Homescreen:** Hit on Safari to launch the web add text field.

    ✓ Copy your message as explained above.

    ✓ Move your finger from the middle bottom of the iPhone in inverted seven $\ulcorner$ to see the minimized **New Message Page**. (go to **Guide Four** learn "How to see reduced app pages")

    ✓ Hit on the New Message Page and follow the above pasting steps.

➤ Once you are through with all the documents attachment, then hit on **Send** ⬆.

# *All You Can Ask Siri To Do For You Through Voice Dictation*

Siri features will help you to organize and properly program your daily, weekly, monthly, and yearly activities successfully.

It is a unique tool iPhone that can help you to operate all the applications on your iPhone quickly and easily. Siri can help you activate any app or control on your iPhone.

Siri can supply you with all current information happening around the world; it could tell you the climatic condition as the moment, traffic condition, reminding you every important saved event in your organizer or calendar.

Siri could help you set alarm when you ask it to do so. It can change your dictated message to a text message and send it to the instructed contact. It can translate the English language to any other language like French, German, Spanish... and more others.

It can help you locate a place on a Google map and show you the bearing compass to get the place. It can assist you to find out a review or reputation about an organization or person.

Siri can tell you where you can locate your favorites using iPhone that you have already registered with Siri. It could help you forward calls to your acquainted favorites or anyone in your contact... many other benefits.

When you call Siri, you will hear a human voice that could be a female or male voice. It depends on the types of sex voice you choose during Siri Setup.

However, for you to know all that Siri could do on your iPhone for you.

# How You Can Effectively Make Siri To Serve You

For Siri to work on your iPhone you must first and foremost finish the setup in the settings, if you have not done it during the iPhone Automatic Setup or Manual Setup.

**Homescreen:** Hit on **Settings**

**Settings:** Move down to select **Siri & Search**

**Siri & Search:** Put On all the below **Activation Buttons** and select your preferable features for each option.

- ➢ Listen for "Hey Siri".
- ➢ Press Side Button for Siri.
- ➢ Allow Siri When Locked.
- ➢ Language.
- ➢ Siri Voice.
- ➢ Voice Feedback.
- ➢ My Information.
- ➢ **SIRI SUGGESTIONS**
  - ✓ Suggestion in Search
  - ✓ Suggestions in Lock Up

**Lock Screen or Homescreen:**

- ➢ Unlock the iPhone (If you did not activate " When Locked")
- ➢ Press the Switch, Sleep, or Wake Button at the right side of your iPhone. (If you have activated "Press Side Button for Siri")
- ➢ **Say:** Hey Siri! What can Siri do
- ➢ Siri will respond and show you all things that it could do.

**You can also use Apple Earpods to call the attention of Siri**

- ➢ Click the Answering middle button to call Siri's attention.

> ➤ Say: Hey Siri!
> ➤ Immediately Siri will answer you. Siri is very sensitive to "Hey Siri", and then continue with your question.

## *How You Can Perfectly Use Safari App*

Safari App on your iPhone makes use of Cellular Service and Wi-Fi Network Data to facilitate the efficiency, however, without network and data you cannot access Safari App.

The use of the Safari app will give the privilege of visiting many websites and move from a webpage to another webpage to gather several details or facts online.

Safari suggests a more related website that you can get more useful messages and also display all the favorite websites.

You can download or save apps through the Safari browser on your iPhone into My iPhone or iCloud drive. The Safari browsing window is loaded with many beneficial tools like:

> ➤ **Page Icon:** To move from webpage to another webpage ▢
>    - ✓ **Add New Tab (Add Icon +)** to add more **Tab**
>    - ✓ **Private** to open a confidential browsing window.
>    - ✓ **Close Icon** to delete the page at the top left edge ✗
>    - ✓ **Done**
> ➤ **Share Icon** to send a page to other apps like Mail, Message, Add to Notes, Bookmark, Reading List, etc.; or to social media page which will be displayed the options of where you can save the webpage. Check any of the below options to determine what format the document will be sent:
>    - ✓ **Automatic:** It will select the exact appropriate format for every application or action
>    - ✓ **PDF**
>    - ✓ **Web Archive**

- ➤ **Download Icon** to access the recent download files on Safari. ⊕
- ➤ **URL with A Small and A Big (AA)**: Small A is used to reduce the font size and the big A is to increase the font size. It is designed to enable the following settings:
  - ✓ Small A Font Size Settings
  - ✓ Big A Size Settings
  - ✓ Show Reader View ▤
  - ✓ Hide Toolbar ↖↘
  - ✓ Request Desktop Website 🖥
  - ✓ Website Settings ⊚

### How to Put the Safari Settings in Place

**Homepage:** Hit on **Settings**.

**Settings**: Scroll down the screen and hit on **Safari**

**Safari**

- ➤ **SEARCH**
  Allow Safari to access Siri by tapping on **Siri & Search** and Activate the switch.
- ➤ **SEARCH**
  - ✓ **The Search Engine** will select your preferable source e.g. Google.
  - ✓ Put On the **Searching Engine Suggestions** Activator.
  - ✓ Put On the **Safari Suggestions** Activator.
  - ✓ Hit on **Quick Website Search** to select **On**
  - ✓ Put On the **Preload Top Hit** Activator.
- ➤ **GENERAL**
  - ✓ Activate **Autofill**
  - ✓ Put On the **Frequency Visited Sites** Activator.
  - ✓ Put On the **Favorite** Activator
  - ✓ Hit on **Favorites** to select **Favorites**
  - ✓ Put On the **Block Pop-up** Activator
  - ✓ Put On the **Show Link Previews** Activator

- ✓ Hit on **Download** to select the storage source e.g. My iPhone and iCloud.
- ➢ **TABS**
  - ✓ Put On **Show Tab Bar** Activator
  - ✓ If you want Icons to be shown in the Tab then you may put On **Show Icons in Tabs'** activation button.
  - ✓ Hit on **Open Links** to select **In New Tab**
  - ✓ Hit on **Close Tabs** to select when you want the open tabs to be closed automatically by Safari. (e.g. Manually, After One Day, After One Week or After One Month).
- ➢ **PRIVACY & SECURITY**
  - ✓ Put On **Prevent Cross-Site Tracking** activator.
  - ✓ Do not activate **Block All Cookies** because they cannot transmit viruses and your iPhone details cannot be hacked by the network hackers.
  - ✓ Put On **Fraudulent Websites Warning'**s activator
  - ✓ Put On **Check for Apple Pay** activator: it will enable you to if the Apple Pay activated and if you are having an Apple Account.
- ➢ **Clear History and Website Data:** If you hit this option you will be able to clear all the browsing history and website data on your iPhone.
- ➢ **SETTING FOR WEBSITE**
  - ✓ Hit on **Page Zoom** for selection between 50%-300% but you may choose 100% for the normal setting.
  - ✓ Hit on **Request Desktop Website** for selection of Websites.
  - ✓ Hit on **Reader** for selection
  - ✓ Hit on **Camera** for selection of Image Size.
  - ✓ Hit on **Microphone** for selection
- ➢ **READING LIST**
  - ✓ You can activate **Automatically Save Offline** if you want all reading lists in the iCloud to be automatically saved.
  - ✓ Hit on **Advance** for selection.

# How To Start Safari Browsing Benefit on Your iPhone

**Homescreen:** Hit on **Safari Icon** at the lower bar menu of the page.

**Safari:**

➢ Hit on the **Browsing Text Field** to type in your searching words from the appeared keyboard.
  ✓ You may select from the predictive dropdown keywords.
  ✓ You may also type your **web address** directly if you are very sure about it.
➢ Hit on the "**Go**" button on your keyboard and what you are looking for will come up.
  If you are searching for social media applications like Facebook, WhatsApp... and many others then hit on the app or hit on the download option if you want to download on your iPhone.
  For **Webpage**: Once the page is displayed "you want to save the page as **Bookmark** for future or reference purpose".
  ✓ Hit on **Bookmark Icon** at the bottom of the page.

  ✓ Select **Add Bookmark for 3 Tabs** on the informative dialog box to **Save** it inside a **New Folder.**

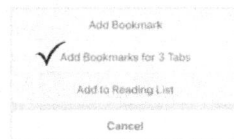

  Add Bookmark
  ✓ Add Bookmarks for 3 Tabs
  Add to Reading List
  Cancel

  ✓ **New Folder:** Give the **Web Tab** a Name, hit on **Done** and it will be saved in the Favorite browsing tabs.
  ✓ If you want to open the web tab later. Hit on Bookmark and select the Name of the web tab and the page will open.

➢ **About Favorites:** These are the websites you visit often and automatically displayed below your Safari browsing search field.

- ✓ You can just hit on any of the come web icons to directly launch the webpage of the website without you retyping the website address into the search field machine.
- ✓ It is very easy and pretty cool to use.
- ✓ If still want to open another website, all you need to do is to hit on **Add New Tab** Icon at the right bottom of the screen. ┼
- ✓ A new page with your favorite websites will be displayed then hit on the other website to also launch another webpage for you to access easily.

➢ **Move From Tab Page To Tab Page**
- ✓ Hit on the Switch Page Icon at the last right bottom of the screen.
- ✓ You will see all the open pages filed up behind one another. With the help of your finger slightly swipe down to reselect any of the pages by tapping on the page.
- ✓ **Delete Tab Page:** Look at the top left edge of each page you will see **Cancel Icon**, tap on it and the tab page will be deleted.

➢ **Other Places You Can Save Your Place** ⬆
- ✓ Hit on the **Share Icon** to access the various apps that you can choose and save the web tap, as mentioned above.

➢ **Use Share Icon to Transfer Webpage from Your iPhone to Another Apple Device** ⬆
- ✓ Go to the bottom of the page and hit on the **Share icon.**
- ✓ Select on **AirDrop** Icon
- ✓ Locate the Apple device **Name** and select. On the other Apple device hit **Accept** on the informative dialog box; instantly you will see the **Webpage** on the other Apple device screen.

## What You Can Do When Webpage Is Not Loading on Safari or Safari Not Responding

There are major technical problems that could prevent Safari from not responding or failed to load the webpage.

1. **Wi-Fi Network:** First and foremost ensure that there is an effective network of the Wi-Fi connection on your iPhone.
   - ✓ **Problem 1:** If your Wi-Fi network is perfectly connected and there is no visible network indication on your iPhone.
   - ✓ **Solution 1:** Relocate yourself to a place where you can see the Wi-Fi network because the stronger the Wi-Fi network the more Safari will be efficiently responding to the loading webpage.

**Full Network**

**Poor Network**

**No Network**

### How to Reactivate the Wi-Fi Network in Setting

**Homescreen:** Hit on **Settings Icon**

**Settings:** Select **Wi-Fi**

**Wi-Fi:** Put Off the **Wi-Fi** Activator 40secs and re-put it On. Go back to Settings and select **Mobile Data.**

**Mobile Data:** Put Off the **Mobile Data** Activator for a 40secs and re-put it On. Go back to Settings and select **General**

**General:** Select **Reset**

**Reset**

> ➤ Select **Reset Network Settings**
> ➤ Hit on the **Enter Password** that will show below.

**Enter Password:** Type in the **Password** and confirm the **Safari.**

## Second Possible Problem

- ✓ **Problem 2:** If you are having s strong Wi-Fi network and Safari is not responding or loading a webpage.
- ✓ **Solution 2:** Crosscheck the Safari settings as some had been stated above and while the rest will be discussed below under **Settings.**

2. **Settings Crosschecking:** Initially go through all the Safari Settings above. Move a little further by tapping on **Advanced** to confirm the various activations Safari Settings.

Homescreen: Hit on **Settings Icon**

Settings: Scroll down to select **Safari**

Safari: Start verifying the activated buttons one by one till you get to **Advanced**. Hit on the **Advanced.**

**Advanced:** Hit on each activation button to put Off and put On again. If you have not activated the below features on your iPhone before ensure that you activate them all because they are very important.

- ✓ **Advanced:** Initially turn Off the feature one by one to confirm the Safari response, if it is working fine. But, if it is not yet responding put On the feature and repeat the same action on the next feature till you get the one that is responsible for the Safari abnormality.
  - Re-put On the **JavaScript** activation button.
  - Select **Experimental Features.**
- ✓ **Experimental WebKit Features**
  - Turn Off & Turn On **Blank anchor target implies...** activation button.
  - Turn Off & Turn On **Fetch API Request KeepAlive ...** activation button.
  - Turn Off & Turn On **Quirk to prevent delayed initial pain...** activation button.
  - Turn Off & Turn On **Intersection Observer...** activation button.

- Turn Off & Turn On **Media Capabilities Extensions** activation button.
- Turn Off & Turn On **Pointer Events** activation button.
- Re-put On **Swap Processes on Cross-Site...** activation button.
- Turn Off & Turn On **Synthetic Editing Commands** activation button.
- Turn Off & Turn On **Block top-level redirects by third...** activation button.
- Turn Off & Turn On **Visual Viewport API** activation button.
- Turn Off & Turn On **WebRTC H264 Simulcast** activation button.
- Turn Off & Turn On **WebRTC mDNS ICE Candidates** activation button.
- Turn Off & Turn On **WebRTC Unified Plan** activation button.
- Turn Off & Turn On the **WebRTC VP8** activation button.
- Turn Off & Turn On **Disable Web SQL** activation button.

# GUIDE EIGHT

## Best Ways of Using Camera and Photo Apps on Your iPhone XS and XS Max

You can use the Camera app to access capture and take pictures of every image around you. The Camera is designed to take a live picture and modified compressed Panorama images. All the captured photographs are automatically saved in Photo Library.

What you could see on the face of the Camera are *a flash icon, live photo icon, timer icon, filter icon, viewfinder, zoom icon, camera modes, thumbnail, shutter, and camera turning icon (rotator).*

### General Features

Flash Icon
Live Photo Icon
Timer Icon
Filter Icon
Viewfinder
Zoom Size Icon
Camera Modes
Shutter
Camera Turning Icon (Rotator)
Thumbnail View

### How to swipe between Camera Modes

The camera has seven different modes of taking an image on your iPhone. The seven Camera modes are:

1. Time Lapse
2. Slo-Mo (Slow Motion)
3. Video
4. Photo
5. Portrait
6. Square
7. Pano (Panorama).

126

**Homescreen**: When you hit on **Camera icon** the Camera will open to **Photo Mode** in the middle of the 7 modes.

If you are to select other modes from **Phone mode**, you have to swipe over from either right to left or left to right for you to access other Camera modes.

When you swipe left (i.e. swipe screen from right to left), you will see the following modes accordingly: **Portrait, Square, and Pano.**

But, when you swipe right from Phone mode at the center of the modes, you will see the following modes: **Video, Slo-Mo, and Time Lapse.**

| CAMERA MODES | | | | | | |
| --- | --- | --- | --- | --- | --- | --- |
| TIME LAPSE | SLO-MO | VIDEO | PHOTO | PORTRAIT | SQUARE | PANO |

## *The importance of Telephoto Camera*

iPhone XS and XS Max came with Dual (Two) Back Camera as they have been previously discussed under the introduction.

The back-facing dual cameras are:

1. *Standard Wide Angle Camera of 12MP f/1.8.*
2. *Telephoto Camera of 12 MP f/2.4.*

1. *Telephoto Camera* will enable you to optically zoom in image two times (2x) when you tap on ⑴ˣ zoom icon at the bottom of the Viewfinder without losing the original quality of

Standard Wide Camera 1x
(Primary Camera)

Telephoto Camera 2x
(Secondary Camera)

the image.

*Hint: If you have your view in one time (1x) zoom you are using a normal standard camera which is called a **Primary Camera,** but if you zoom in the image 2x you have a chance to a Telephoto camera which is the **Secondary Camera.***

2. ***Telephoto Camera*** will also enable to effectively use Portrait light effect options on your Photograph. When you swipe the Viewfinder from right to left (left swipe/swipe over) to select **Portrait view**.

The portrait will let you select the focus point of the image by tapping the major part of the image for your camera to focus.

When you make the focus point a white square will appear to surround the target part of the image.

The surrounding light of the focused object will gain different background colors which are known as **Focus Effect.**

*Hint:* When you hit on a box frame containing a ball inside for **Normal** light of Portrait lighting mode in an anticlockwise direction to select other light modes, the camera will switch to the Telephoto Camera to add different light effects (focus effects) around the image.

The Portrait Lighting Mode is *Natural, Studio, Contour, and Stage, Stage Mono.*

**Second Light Mode** — STUDIO LIGHT

**Fourth Light Mode** — STAGE LIGHT

**Third Light Mode** — CONTOUR LIGHT

**Fifth Light Mode** — STAGE MONO LIGHT

# How You Can Control Exposure of Your Image

You can reduce the brightness or darkness of the screen image by:

> ➢ Tapping on the image to show a focus square at the surface.
> ➢ Place your finger at the side of the Viewfinder move your finger up to increase the brightness of the Camera.
> ➢ When you move your finger down you will increase the darkness of the Viewfinder of the Camera.

**Second Method**

> ➢ On the **Photo Mode:** Press down the focus image on the screen for **AE (Autoexposure)/AF (Autofocus) LOCK** label to appear at the top center of the Viewfinder.

This implies that the automatic exposure and focus control of the Camera has been locked.

> ➢ Press and hold anywhere on the Viewfinder around the focused image remove the location focus and exposure. This will enable the surrounding of the image to look brighter.

## *To Restore AE/AF of Your Camera*

➤ Hit on the **Image** and the AE/AF Locked will be canceled.

**How You Can Add Effect On Image Before Taking**

Photo Mode

➤ Select **Filter Icon** at the top right corner of the screen ⬤. When the Filter is selected it will change to this look ⬤

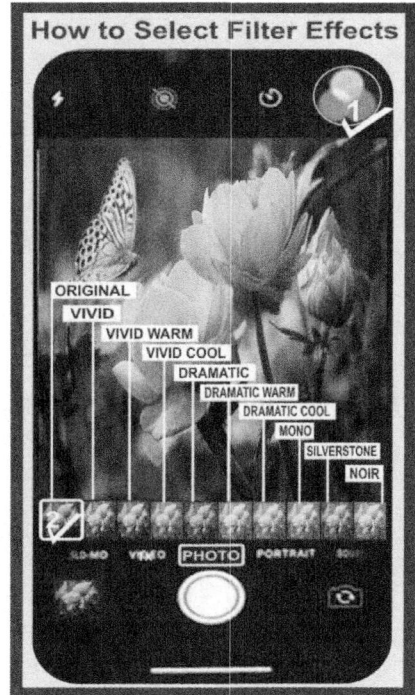

How to Select Filter Effects

ORIGINAL
VIVID
VIVID WARM
VIVID COOL
DRAMATIC
DRAMATIC WARM
DRAMATIC COOL
MONO
SILVERSTONE
NOIR

➤ At the bottom of the Viewfinder, you will see a file up squares containing the image you about to snap with different effects. Hit on each square image to choose a more lovely color effect. This is the following Filer Effects: ORGINAL, VIVID, VIVID WARM, VIVID COOL, DRAMATIC, DRAMATIC WARM, DRAMATIC COOL MONO, SILVERTONE, and NOIR.

➤ Take your shot and re-tap the Filter icon at the top right of the screen to deactivate it.

## *How to Use Filter Options for Saved Photos*

Photo

➤ Hit on **Thumbnail** at the bottom left of the screen, beside **Shutter.**

➤ Select a photo that you wanted to add filter effect.

➤ Hit on the **Filter icon** at the top right angle of the screen.

131

➢ Scroll through the different color effects to select your choice.
➢ Hit on the Save option to save the edited photo.

**Other Method**

Homescreen: Hit on **Photo** icon to launch the Photo page

Photo Page:

➢ You can select **Portrait** or **Album** at the bottom menu of the screen to tap on the picture you are looking for.
➢ On the Picture page tap on **Edit** to select **Filter.**
➢ Select the filter effect and hit on **Done** to save the edited photo.

## *How to Use Timer to Take Pictures*

Homescreen: Hit on the **Camera icon**

Photo Mode

➢ Hit on the **Timer icon** at the top of the screen. [icon]

➢ Select the seconds you would like to delay shutter action before taking your picture. You can either tap 3s (seconds) or 10s. If you select 3 or 10 seconds, the time will complete before the camera takes the picture.
➢ Hit on **Shutter** below.
➢ Allow the time to countdown and the shot will be taken.

Hint: You can select 3s or 10s for you to fix the iPhone on a Phone stand and position yourself in front of the Camera or join a group picture or take a personal picture.

Timing Photo Shot
Step 1
Step 2
Step 3
Step 4

Countdown

**How to take Live Photo**

Homescreen: Hit on the **Camera icon**

Photo Mode

➤ Hit on **Live** icon at the top right side of the Camera interface, the icon will change to yellow and you will see LIVE at the top center of the page. . 🔘 Off, 🔘 On,

➤ Let the Camera capture image correctly within a rectangle that is automatically showing at the center of the view of fame or Grid.

➤ Hit on **Shutter** to take a shot of the image.

The Image will be saved in the Photo library as Live Photo

Hint: Ensure the Live icon is off before you take a normal Photo. Otherwise, the photo will be a few second delayed and faster than normal to display slight movement when touched

**How You Could Use Flash on Camera to Take Photos**

Homescreen: Hit on **Camera icon** ⚡

Photo Mode

➤ Look at the top left of the screen to hit on the **Flash icon.**

➤ Hit on any of the following options:

  ✓ **Auto:** This will automatically display flash (light) when the background of the image is dark during every Photo snap you take.

  ✓ **On:** This will always come-up anytime you select the On option.

  ✓ **Off:** When you tap the Off option it will disable the effect of the flash.

➤ Hit on the **Flash icon** to close the options menu. ⚡

**Use Burst Shot for Multiple Photo Shots at a Goal**

It will enable you to take a continuous photo shot that you can later select the nice pictures among the total shots.

Camera Interface

> ➢ Let your iPhone Camera be positioned at the image.
> ➢ Press down the **Shutter** till you have completely taken a **lot of Photos** of an image at a time. The number of Photos will show above the Shutter. Once you remove your finger from the Shutter, it will stop.
> ➢ Hit the **Thumbnail** at the left side of the Shutter to see all the multiple pictures you have taken.
> ➢ Hit on **Select** to select the most perfect looking picture(s).
> ➢ Hit on **Done** at the top right corner of the screen when you are satisfied.
> ➢ Hit **Keep Only 1 Favorite** (if you have selected one**).**

# *How to Record Video or Slo-Mo at the Highest Efficiency*

The Video mode is similar to Slo-Mo processes. The output of the Video will be accurate with the original movement without any delay.

At the top right angle of the screen, you will see HD-60 which means that your Camera video recording has been set to a high definition of 1080p at 60 frames per second by default.

To have the best of the Normal Video and Slo-Mo Video production on your iPhone with the highest quality resolution and efficiency of 4K at 60fps, you have to initially do the following settings before you start the recording.

Homescreen: Hit on **Settings Icon**

Settings: Select **Camera**

Camera: Hit on **Record SLO-MO**

**Record SLO-MO:** Select **1080p HD** at **240fps** (frame per second), return to **Camera** settings by hitting on **Back Icon** at the top left of the screen

Camera: Hit on **Record Video**

**Record Video**

> Select **4k at 60fps**.
> Hit on **Back Icon** to return to **Camera** settings.

Camera: Hit on **Format**

**Format:** Hit on **High Efficiency**

> Swipe up from the bottom to go back to the **Homescreen.**

Homescreen: Hit on **Camera App Icon**

Camera Interface: You

How to Improve the Speed & Efficacy of Video Recording

135

will see the efficiency changed to 4K – 60 at the top right side of the iPhone.

➢ Select **Video** from the Camera Modes below View margin.
➢ Hit on the Red Recording Button to **Start** the recording.
➢ Hit on the button again to Stop the **Video Recording.**

## Slo-Mo (Slow Motion)

You can apply motion with a timer to beautify modeling, sports activities, production stages, advertisement, growth... and many others.

Camera Interface: Below the View-frame scroll the Camera mode and hit on **Slo-Mo.**

➢ Position your iPhone either in Portrait or Landscape the best way you want it.
➢ Hit on the Red Recording Button at the bottom center to start your **Selfie Slo-Mo recording** on your Camera.
➢ Hit on the Red Recording Button again to Stop the **Slo-Mo Recording.**
➢ **To Play Your Recorded Slo-Mo:** Go to Homescreen and hit on **Photo App.**
➢ Hit on the Slo-Mo and it will play. You can share with your friends in iMessage, Social Media by tapping **Share Icon** at the bottom of the screen.
   ✓ **To Share:** Select the **Recorded Slo-Mo**
   ✓ Hit on **Share Icon** below. 
   ✓ Select any of the locations you wanted to send it to.

   **OR**

   **When you are composing text on iMessage**

   ✓ At the top left of the Keyboard tap on Photo icon

   ✓ Scroll down to tap Video and select the **Slo-Mo.**
   ✓ Hit on Send Icon.

Hint: You can also select Photo from either Recent Photo or All Photo and send it on iMessage.

## *How You Could Use Pano Mode (Panorama)*

Homescreen: Hit on **Camera Icon**

Camera Interface

- ➢ Look at the lower base of the Viewfinder Frame scroll from either left to right or right to left to hit on **Pano.**
- ➢ First, let the Camera capture the left end of the image.
- ➢ View it in the rectangle Image View
- ➢ Hit on Shutter to start capture
- ➢ Slowly move your hand straight from the left edge side of the Image to the right edge side of the image. Use the Arrow on a straight line to guide your straight movement.
- ➢ Hit on the same Shutter to stop the shot.
- ➢ The Image will be spherically wide in size and look beautiful.
- ➢ You can also use it to make Selfies in the same method.

**How to remove vertical & horizontal lines on your Camera screen**

The line is very useful for you to properly position your image at the center of the Camera's Viewfinder. But if you do not need it, then go to:

Homescreen: Hit on the **Settings** icon.

Settings: Select **Camera**

Camera

- ➢ Hit on the **Grid** activation switch to deactivate it. The switch will change from green to white as it was shown above.
- ➢ Swipe Up to go back Home.

137

Homescreen: Hit on the **Camera icon**

Camera: On the Camera's Viewfinder you will not see the lines (Grid) again. But if you later want the line to reappear on the screen, then go back to the above steps of deactivation to hit on the **Grid** activation switch to change from white to green.

Hint: If you snapped an image when the grid is on the screen, the lines will not appear on the snapped picture. It is used as a guide.

# How to Use Your iPhone Camera to Scan Quick Response (QR) Code

Quick Response (QR) Code activation will enable your camera to scan QR code that will allow you to go to a website without you typing the *web address* on your iPhone browser **web tab** of Safari.

First and foremost you have to activate the function in the Camera Settings to enable the QR Code recognizing feature.

**How to Activate the Camera QR Code Scanner**

Homescreen: Hit on the **Settings** icon.

Settings: Select **Camera**

Camera

➢ Hit on the **Scan QR Code** activation switch to activate it. . The switch will change from white to green.
➢ Swipe Up to go back to Homescreen.

**How you can use the Camera App to Scan the QR Code on your iPhone**

Lock Screen or Homescreen or Control Center: Hit on the **Camera icon**

Camera

138

> Ensure that you are using the Rear (Back) Camera. If not, hit on Camera turning icon (rotator)  at the bottom right of the screen to turn the camera view to the rear Camera.
> Position your camera to focus on the Quick Response Code.
> A notification will show up on your screen for you to open the **Website** link (e.g. Open "amazon.com" in Safari).

**Notification**

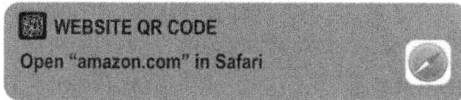

> Hit on the notification to open the website link with the **Quick Response**.

## *How to Use High Dynamic Range (HDR) Camera to Produce Outstanding Photo Shoots*

The use of High Dynamic Range (HDR) will make your pictures look more colorful, real, and attractive.

It could enable **Automatically** or **Manually.** When the camera is set to Auto HDR every Photoshoot that will be taken will be automatically beautified with perfect color and awesome effect.

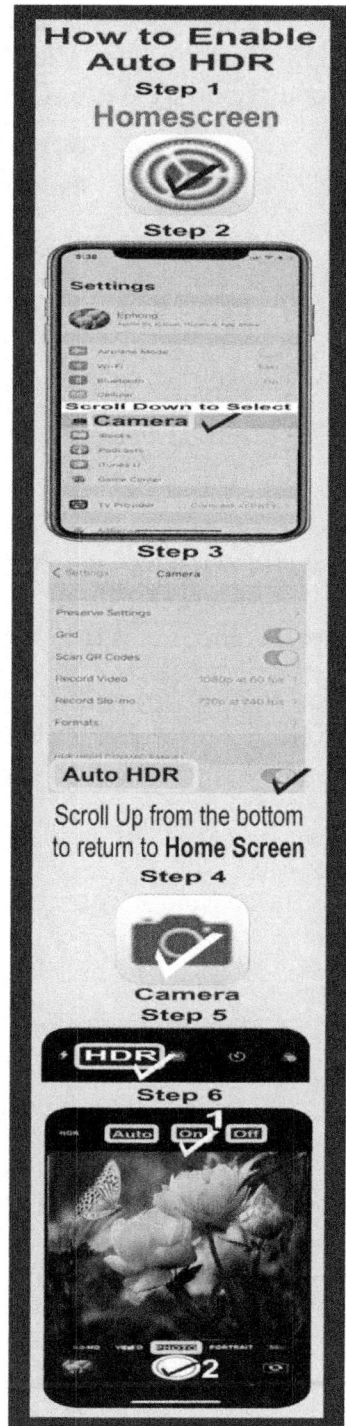

139

But if you disable Auto HDR, you will see the option of HDR at top of the Viewfind for you to tap and select from the menu including **Auto, On,** and **Off**.

**HDR   Auto   On   Off**

If you select the **On** option before you take any picture, you have to enable the manual function of the HDR effect on the picture. **HDR**

When you select the **Off** option from the menu then you have disabled the function of HDR on every picture that you will be taken after. **HDR**

But, if you select the **Auto** option that means you have manually chosen Auto HDR which could be also off by tapping on the HDR menu at the top of the Viewfinder.

However, if you prefer having the HDR option to be permanently fixed to Auto HDR without showing the icon at the top menu, then you have to Settings to get it done.

Homescreen: Hit on the **Settings** icon

Settings: Select **Camera**

Camera

> ➢ Hit on the **Auto HDR** activation switch to change to green.

> ➢ Swipe Up to go back to **Homescreen**

Homescreen: Launch your **Camera** by tapping on the Camera icon.

Start taking your pictures. All your pictures will be automatically enhanced with high dynamic range color effects and come out pretty good.

**How To Backup All The Saved Pictures With iCloud Photo Library**

This will quickly save all your photos and video iCloud storage to prevent total loss when your iPhone is lost or suddenly develops a technical problem that may cause your iPhone to delete all the documents on it. But, since they have been saved in the iCloud Photo Library, you could recover all back on your iPhone completely.

Homescreen: Hit on the **Settings** icon

Settings: Select **Photo**

Photo: Hit on **iCloud Photo Library** activation switch to change to green, .

Swipe up from the bottom center to return to **Homescreen.**

Homescreen: Press the Siri button and ask Siri:

Hey Siri! Show me all Photos that were taken yesterday

Immediately, all the pictures you took yesterday will display for you to see on your screen.

**How to permit Siri to search Photos on your iPhone**

When you enable Siri to always search for any particular photo for you on the iPhone, it will quickly provide all the requested Photos within a second.

Homescreen: Hit on the **Settings** icon

Settings: Select **Photo**

Photo

➢ Hit on **Siri & Search**

141

➤ Hit on **Search & Siri Suggestions** activation switch to change to green,

*On the same page of PHOTO you can activate the following options to improve easy accessibility:*

1. **iCloud Photo Sharing** : This will create albums to share with other people, or subscribe to other people's shared albums.

2. **Summarize Photos** : The Photos tab will show every photo in your library in all views. You can choose compact, summarized views for Collection and Year.

3. **View Full HDR** : It will automatically adjust the display to show the complete dynamic range of Photos.

4. **Show Holiday Events** : **Under Memory,** this will enable you to see holiday event for your Home Country.

5. **Automatic:** Under Transfer to MAC or PC, you can tap this option also to be checked in order to automatically transfer Photos and Video in a compatible format, or always transfer the original file without checking for compatibility.

6. Select **Keep Original.**

**Hint:** Do not enable Cellular Data to download Photos or Videos, therefore, deactivate the activation switch of **Cellular Data** when you tap on it. This will save your cellular data from being used up quickly.

Always use a Wi-Fi network connection to download photos and videos by going to Control Center and select Wi-Fi Icon.

# *How You Can Use Professional Camera App To Boost Your Photograph Quality*

If you want to be using your iPhone professional photography then you will need to know to control the Picture(s) Manual Shutter Speed, ISO, Exposure... and many others, for you to get an amazing outstanding picture(s)

Therefore, you will download an additional Camera App called **ProCamera** that will enable you to have access to a menu that contains many editing tools you could use to improve the general quality of the Photo.

When you launch the ProCamera App, it will show the normal Camera App look with advanced feature of exposure control under Viewfinder for you to regulate the picture exposure to be brighter or darker when you place your finger on the **Zero (O)** Calibrated Pointer and slide the control pointer toward the right to increase the exposure brightness or toward the left to increase the exposure darkness.

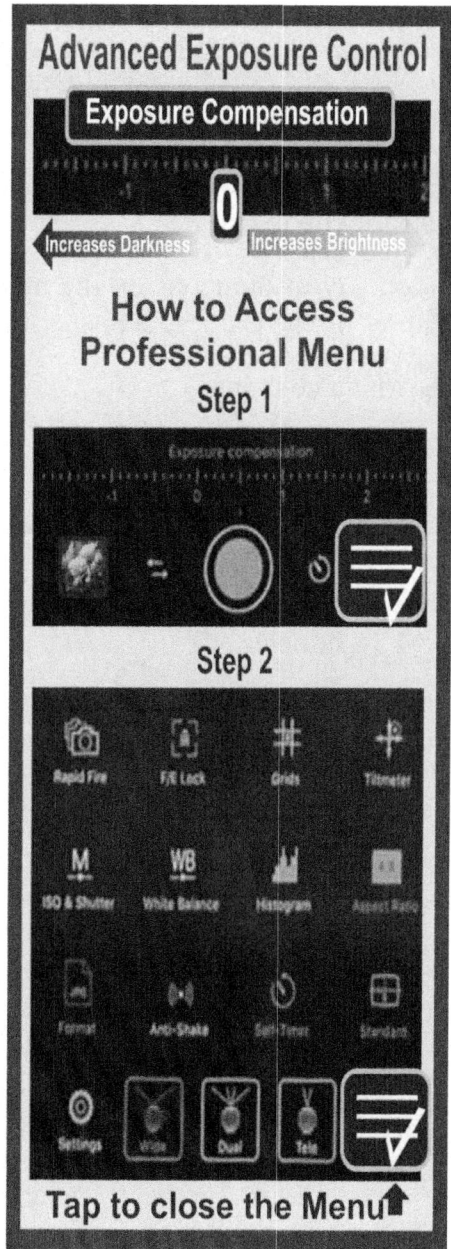

**How to Access Professional Menu**

After you have downloaded ProCamera on your iPhone.

**Homescreen:** Hit on ProCamera App.

**On the Camera Interface:** Look at the bottom left of the screen to hit on the **Menu icon.** ☰

The hidden menu will display all the available advanced effect tools for you to use.

Hit on any of the icons on the menu. It will show the icon and its features on the Camera screen.

The Menu contains:

1. Rapid Fire 📷
2. F/E (Focus Point and Exposure) Locked 🔒
3. Grids ▦
4. Tiltmeter ⊕
5. ISO & Shutter Ⓜ
6. White Balance WB
7. Histogram 📊
8. Aspect Ratio ▱
9. JPEG Format 🄹
10. Anti-Shake ⊙
11. Self Timer 🕐
12. Standard ▦
13. Settings ◎

**1. Rapid Fire:** The feature of Rapid Fire is the same as the feature of the Burst method of taking many pictures within a very short time by pressing and hold the Shutter.

## ProCamera Menu

> ➢ Hit on the Menu icon
> ➢ Hit on the **Rapid Fire** icon
> ➢ Go down to the bottom right of the menu to tap on the Menu icon. This will hide all the menu effect tools.
> ➢ Position your Camera to the Image you want to snap, press, and hold the Shutter to snap the number of shots you want.

2. **Focus Point and Exposure (E/F) Lock:** This feature is used to lock the focus point and exposure level you preferred for the picture.

## ProCamera Menu

> ➢ Position your Camera to the image you want to snap.
> ➢ Hit the surface of the Viewfinder for both Focus Point and Exposure Shapes to appear on the screen.
> ➢ On the Viewfinder, you will see focus points in a square shape and exposure in a circular shape. With the use of your finger move the square shape to the area that should be sharp on the viewfinder, and move the circle to the area where the exposure is needed to be corrected.
> ➢ Use the control below to regulate the exposure and the focus as you move your finger on the controlling panel.
> ➢ Hit on the Menu icon at the bottom right of the screen to display the editing tools.

F/E Lock Mode
Step 1

Step 2

145

- Select F/E Lock icon
- Hit on Menu icon at the bottom right to hide the effect tools.
- Now you can move your Camera anywhere and how to capture different shots without any irregularity.
- As soon as you have finished taking Photos go to the menu and hit on the **F/E Lock** icon to disable it. The **F/E Lock** icon will appear white when it is disabled but lemon green when it is enabled (active).

Hint: If you move your Camera before you select **F/E Lock** from the Menu the focus and exposure setting will change.

3. **Grids:** The advanced grids are more compact than the grids in the ordinary Camera App. It can be used to centralize a very small image that could not be done with the other grids on the Camera app.

ProCamera Menu

- Hit on the Menu icon at the bottom right
- Select **Grids** icon
- Hit on the Menu icon
- Use the squares on the viewfinder to set your image.
- Hit on Shutter to take the Picture.
- You can go back to Menu to disable the active Grids icon.

4. **Tiltmeter:** This will enable you to balance the Camera of your iPhone. The cross icon shows if the image is correctly positioned.

ProCamera Menu

- Hit on the Menu icon at the bottom right
- Select **Tiltmeter** icon

146

➢ Hit on the Menu icon

➢ Use the Tiltmeter (Big Cross) on the viewfinder
to be in line with the small cross and when it is
correctly registered on each other the Tiltmeter will turn to
**Green**.

➢ Hit on Shutter to take the Picture.

➢ You can go back to Menu to disable the active Tiltmeter
icon.

5. **ISO & Shutter**: This is also called **Manual Mode** that
regulates the speed of Shutter and could be used to control
exposure as it is used in Digital Single-Len Reflex Camera.
The faster the Shutter the more the advantage of producing
a clearer picture with low light.
The higher the number of ISO the more light-sensitive your
iPhone Camera.

ProCamera Menu

➢ Hit on the **Menu icon** at the bottom right

➢ Select **ISO & Shutter** icon

➢ Hit on the Menu icon

➢ At the top of the Viewfinder, you will see Shutter Speed
reading rate **1/3xxx s** and **ISO 4x.** Tap on 1/3xxx

➢ Use the Shutter Speed to control the speed time.

**To Control ISO**

➢ Hit on the **ISO 4x (**e.g ISO 48) at the top right of
the Viewfinder.

➢ Drag the **ISO Sensitivity Regulator** below the Viewfinder
toward the right to increase your iPhone Camera light
sensitivity.

6. **White Balance:** The Picture colors on your Camera are
controlled by color temperature which is known as
additional Blue that is representing Cooler and additional

147

Yellow which is representing Warmer. If you add more of yellow color to your picture that means it is having additional warming temperature while the increase of Blue color on your picture is reducing the temperature of your picture and the temperature is reading in **Kelvin (K)**

 ➤ Hit on the **Menu** icon at the bottom right
 ➤ Select the **White Balance** icon
 ➤ Hit on the Menu icon
 ➤ At the bottom of the Viewfinder hit on **AWB** the reading scale will show.
 ➤ The cooling (Blue) temperature is increasing when you move the Color Temperature Slider toward the left while Warming (Yellow) temperature is increasing when you move the slider toward the right.

Hint: As you are adding blue the temperature reading value will be reducing and as you are adding yellow to the picture the temperature reading value will be increasing.

7. **Histogram**: This is a picture graph that explains the equal exposure level of darkness or brightness pixels on a Picture. It shows if a picture is having high or excessive brightness (i.e. overexposure) or darkness (i.e. underexposure).

 ➤ Hit on the **Menu** icon at the bottom right
 ➤ Select **Histogram** icon
 ➤ Hit on the Menu icon

**Hint:** The right peak side of the picture exposure graph is representing the maximum brightness pixels in the picture.

The middle area of the picture color graph is showing a minimal level of brightness.

The left peak side of the picture exposure graph is representing the optimal level of darkness.

When you either reduce or add exposure to your picture through the use of Exposure Compensation, It will quickly arrange the histogram to show the effects of the picture color pixels.

For You to Remove the Histograph

> Hit on the **Menu** icon at the bottom right
> Hit on the **Histogram** icon to deactivate it. It will change from lemon green to white.
> Hit on the Menu icon to minimize the editing tools.

8. **Anti-Shake:** As the name implies, it prevents the image capture from going through an unconscious and uncontrollable shaking defect when the light is low or poor. It ensures clear and sharp capture of images in a poor light environment.

**Anti-Shake** will automatically switch on itself as soon as the Camera discovered the surrounding light is bad for a good picture. When you launch the **ProCamera App** and go to Menu, you will see the Anti-Shake feature has been automatically switched On to ensure quality Photo.

9. **Aspect Ratio:** This is an interesting ProCamera feature that helps all individuals to print out their photos according to the size of their desirable Photo's Frame.

The ratio measures the breadth and height of the Photo you are about to take. By default, you will see 3:2 on your Camera when you have activated the Aspect Ratio option on the menu.

This option is telling you that the size of the Photo breadth will be 3 while the height will be 2.

Practically, if you want to choose a frame, you will need to understand how to work out the Aspect Ratio first.

Ratio 3:2 means, the breadth is taking the size of 3 out of 5 (3/5 or three-fifth) and the height is taking the size of 2 out of 5 (2/5 or two-fifth)

If you are having the size of the frame, you must calculate the ratio between the breath and the height of the frame.

For instance, 4 inches by 6 inches Frame size

In this contest, a small number (4) comes before the bigger number (6). Any of the sides could be considered breadth or height since the difference between them is ratio 3:2.

How can you know that?

Continue dividing both figures with a common number that could go in them until you are unable to divide them again a common number.

Between 4 and 6 the common number for both is 2

Divide both by 2 = 4/2 = 2; and 6/2 = 3

Now you can conclude that the frame is ratio 2:3 is the same with ratio 3:2.

Let's try another frame size 16 inches by 24 inches (16" x 24")

What are the common numbers (also called a common factor) in both?

Start from the smallest number: 2,4, & 8

Those three numbers could completely divide both sides to last the last number that could not allow any division again.

To safe time, let's use 8

If you divide both numbers by 8 you will get = 16/8 =2; and 24/8 = 3

The fame 16" x 24" is in Aspect Ratio 2:3.

Therefore, the frame could work perfectly for any picture you have taken with an Aspect Ratio 3:2

Now, you can try to find out the ratio of these frame sizes.

1. 8" x 12"
2. 32" x 48" and
3. 64" x 96"

I wish you good luck.

## ProCamera Menu

You can change the Aspect Ratio from default ratio 3:2  to another commonly available of your own choice by tapping on the **Aspect Ratio** icon in the ProCamera Menu.

Every each time you tap the Aspect Ratio it will change to another option of the ratio which includes:

1. 1:1
2. 3:1 Panorama Size.
3. 4:3
4. 5:4
5. 16:9
6. Golden Mean

10. **File Format:** This will help you to compress your pictures to use very small storage space on your iPhone & iCloud when the pictures are saved in JPG/JPEG format.

Ordinarily, your Camera always saves your Photographs in JPEG format to make them compatible and very useful in all devices.

Although, JPEG pictures are compressed photos, meanwhile, in the process of compressing and saving the pictures in JPEG format they partially lose some degree of light which affects the overall quality. However, they are still pretty good to use.

But, with the use of the **ProCamera App** on your iPhone you can effectively use other options of saving your pictures. The other options are TIFF, RAW, and RAW+JPEG.

These options will not compress your Photos as a result, they will be very heavy and take too much of storage space on your iPhone and iCloud.

The advantage is that any picture you save with either TIFF or RAW will 100% protect the degree of the light, total exposure, and come out excellently.

**How to select the File Format of Your Choice**

You may want to save a particular picture in a different file format based on a special request. Take the steps below:

ProCamera Menu

> ➢ Hit on the **Menu** icon at the bottom right
> ➢ Hit on **File Format**, you will first see JPEF; re-tap the icon you will see TIFF and continue tapping it till you see your preferred option.
> ➢ Hit on the Menu icon
> ➢ When you are through, go back to the menu to reset it to the JPEG file.

# GUIDE NINE

## How To Get Your Lost iPhone Back

There are some important steps of settings you have to do on your iPhone which will make the feature of **Find My** active on your iPhone XS or XS Max.

1. Find Friends and Family Members or
2. Share your location with others
3. Set up **Find My.**

**How You Can Activate Find My on Your iPhone**

Hint: **"Find My"** is automatically turned on when you Sign In your new iPhone with your Apple ID, but, there is a need for you to find out if **Find My iPhone, Enable Offline Finding** and **Send Last Location** are activated.

Homescreen: Hit on **Settings**

Settings: Hit on your **Name/Sign In To Your iPhone** beside the profile picture.

Apple ID: Hit on **Find My**

Find My

➢ Hit on **Find My iPhone** to select **"On"** if the activation

153

feature is **Off.**

**Find My iPhone:** Turn On the activators of the following if they are Off:

- ✓ **Find My iPhone:** It will always request your Password to locate, erase, or lock your iPhone.
- ✓ **Enable Offline Finding:** Your iPhone will be located even when it is not connected to a cellular or Wi-Fi network.
- ✓ **Send Last Location:** iCloud will automatically send the location of your iPhone to Apple when the battery is drastically low.
- ➢ Hit on **My Location** to select **This Device.**
- ➢ Hit on **Share My Location's Activator** to put on the switch.

## *What To Do After You Have Lost Your iPhone*

There is a possibility of misplacing your iPhone XS or XS Max in a location that you could not recollect because you had visited more than three places before you could remember that your iPhone is missing or it was stolen by a thief.

Also, you might have kept the iPhone in a compartment that is best known to you only but after a while, you could not remember specifically where exactly you had hidden the iPhone.

However, Apple has made a reliable way of locating your iPhone XS or XS Max with the use of Find My iPhone and iCloud Map Detection or Google Map to specifically describe and identify the location of your iPhone wherever it had been kept.

**First Finding Solution**

**On Mac or PC**

- ➢ Use any of the available browsers such as Chrome, Mozilla Firefox, Internet Explorer, Safari, Opera, Lynx, or Konqueror.
- ➢ In the Web Add text field type **icloud.com.**

**iCloud Homepage:**

154

- ➢ Sign In with your Apple ID which includes your **Email** and **Password**.
- ➢ Click on **Find iPhone Icon** ⚫ among the icons on the screen.

iCloud Find My iPhone: Location Map will display on the screen.

- ➢ At the top **bar** center of the screen click on All Devices.
- ➢ On the **drop-down & select your iPhone**. (If you are using more than one Apple device that is using the same Apple ID. You will see all the Apple devices on the drop-down).
- ➢ The Map will zoom out to indicate the iPhone location with a black circle and your iPhone' Name label
- ➢ At the right corner, you will see 3 options you can use to help your findings
  - ✓ Play Sound
  - ✓ Lost Mode
  - ✓ Erase iPhone

**Play Sound:** If you pretty sure that the iPhone is around (home,

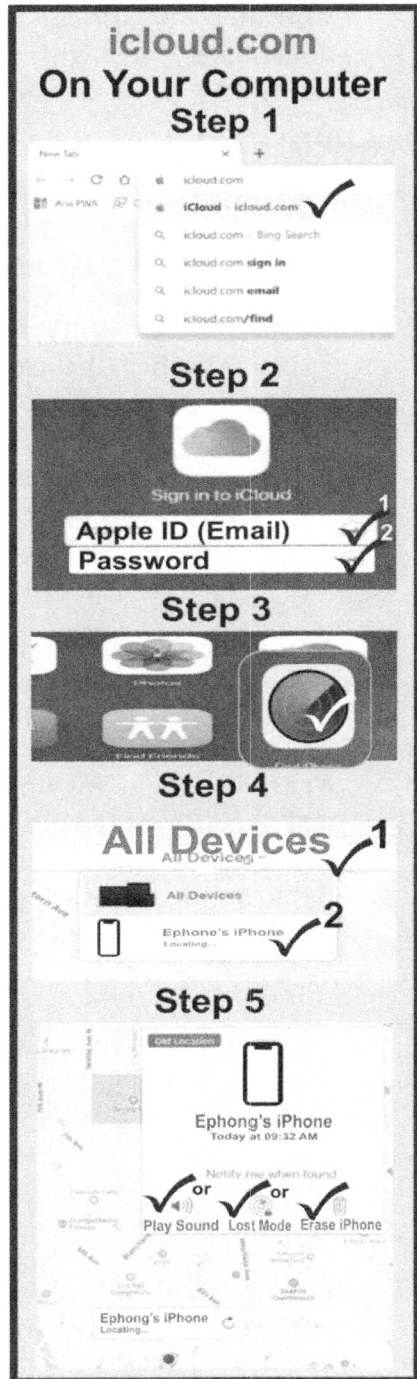

**icloud.com**
**On Your Computer**
**Step 1**

**Step 2**

Sign in to iCloud
Apple ID (Email)
Password

**Step 3**

**Step 4**

**All Devices**
All Devices
Ephone's iPhone
Locating...

**Step 5**

Ephong's iPhone
Today at 09:32 AM

Notify me when found
or        or
Play Sound  Lost Mode  Erase iPhone

Ephong's iPhone
Locating...

155

workshop, or office) then you can click **Play Sound** immediately you will start hearing vibration with sound. The sound will continue until you hit on **Find My iPhone Alert** OK.

**Lost Mode:** This option perfect when you discovered that you can no longer recover/find your iPhone again then you can click on **Lost Mode.**

✓ **Phone Number Dialog Box:** Type your **Phone Number** (that can be called by the finder) and click on **Next** at the top right corner of the dialog box.

✓ Click on the Text box, type the message that will be shown on your iPhone screen. e.g. **"Please I have lost this iPhone. Kindly Call Me. Thank you"** and click on **Done** at the top right angle of the dialog box.

Automatically the iPhone will be locked. It will only be unlocked if you enter your passcode or through your Face ID.

**Erase iPhone:** This option is accurate when you realized that the iPhone could not be located, then, click **Erase iPhone** to completely remove all your vital and confidential **data, applications (apps) & documents** from the iPhone quickly.

**Second Finding Solution:**

This is can be used when you are having Google Map App on your iPhone but if do not have the app you can use the iCloud method above.

On Mac or PC

➢ Use any of the available browsers such as Chrome, Mozilla Firefox, Internet Explorer, Safari, Opera, Lynx, or Konqueror.

➢ In the Web Add text field type **www.google.com/maps**

**Google Maps:**

➢ Click on **Menu Icon** at the top left side of the **Search Google Maps Text Field**.

➢ **Menu:** Select **Your Timeline** (Timeline will show various locations you have been with your iPhone on Google maps with an indication of red color).

➢ At the to left side of the screen click on **Today** at the front of the **Timeline**.

Immediately a line will displace your different movement today on the Google maps to know where your iPhone could be found.

➢ You can zoom in the map to make the location to be closer and clearer for you to see the location very well.

➢ You can increase the displacement line (appear in blue) at the left side of the screen to see more of different places with their specific time in hours, minutes, and seconds that you moved from a particular place to another place till the final place where the iPhone could be found.

Note: You won't see the exact spot where the iPhone could be found on

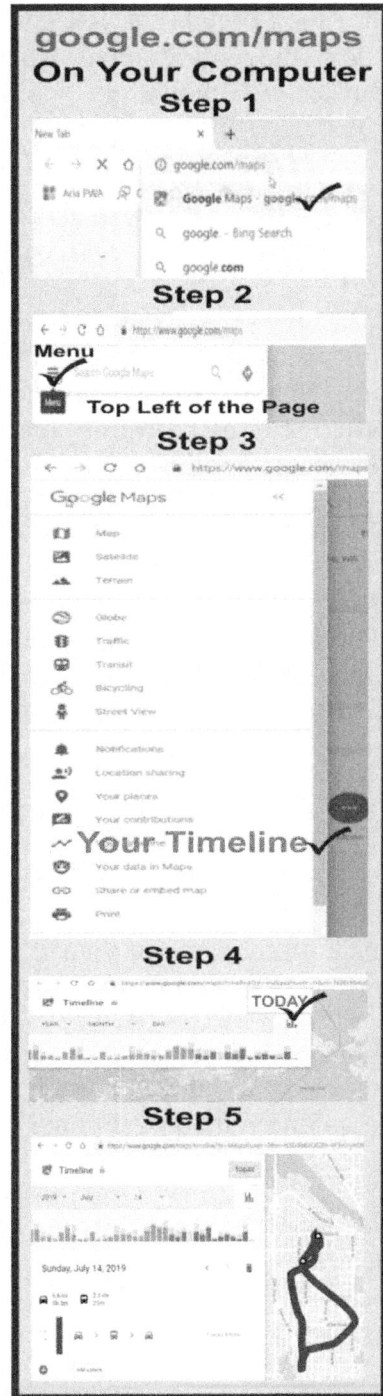

the Google map but you could only know the environment where you can see the iPhone.

## How You Can Use Another iPhone to Track Your Lost iPhone

The method of tracking your lost iPhone on the computer is virtually the same as the method and processes of locating your lost iPhone on another iPhone.

If you are having two iPhones in your family or your friend is have one, you can easily use the available iPhone to quickly discover where your iPhone is kept or the location at which it could be found with either hope of recovery or not.

Homescreen: Hit on **Find My** App Icon

Find My: Hit on **Devices** icon at the bottom center of your iPhone.

Devices: Hit on your lost **iPhone XS's Name** (e.g. Ephong's iPhone) that is your first name will be used to qualified the lost iPhone.

iPhone XS's Name: Swipe up from the top edge center of the page to select one of the available options below:

1. **Play Sound**: Having 100% assurance of finding it.

Use iPhone To Track Step 1

Step 2

People

Start Sharing Location

Step 2a

Step 2b

Share for One Hour
Share Until End of Day
Share Indefinitely
Cancel

Step 2c

You started sharing your location with (The Person's Phone Number)

OK

158

2. **Directions**: If it is discovered on the map and you want it to be tracked down,
3. **Notifications:** You will be notified when the iPhone is found.
4. **Mark As Lost**: If the recovery chances of your iPhone is 70 – 80% but the location on the map displayed is extremely far. Then you can hit on **Active.**
5. **Erase This Device**: If the chance of recovering your iPhone is less than 50% which is very narrow, then you can choose the option by tapping it.

Hint: if you eventually selected **Erase This Device** because you have initially lost hope of finding it, as a result, you would not be able to track your iPhone again. But, if by slim opportunity you found the iPhone, you will only be able to restore all the erased data and documents on your iPhone through iCloud backup.

## *How You Can Share Your Location with Others*

You will need to select the people that you wanted to share your location with. This option will enable you to track down your lost iPhone on your friend's iPhone.

**Homescreen:** Hit on **Find My App Icon**

**Find My:** Hit on **People** icon at the bottom left of the screen.

**People:** Hit on **Start Sharing Location**

**Start Sharing Location**

- ➤ Type the **Name of the Person** you want to share your location into the Text Field and hit on **Send** at the top right angle of the page.
- ➤ An Optional Dialog Box will show up to select "time for the sharing of your location with the person". Select any of the flowing options:
  - ✓ Share for One Hour
  - ✓ Share Until End of Day
  - ✓ Share Indefinitely
- ➤ **Notification:** On a Dialog box you will see "You Shared Your Location with the Person's Contact. Hit on **OK.**

# *How You Can Setup CarPlay Connection on Your iPhone & Car Stereo*

You need to confirm if your car is supporting Apple CarPlay before you start the connection process.

**What to Do First**
- ➤ Confirm the CarPlay compatibility with your Stereo.
- ➤ Verify if the use of CarPlay is allowed in your area or Country.
- ➤ Start your car, let the screen stereo boot, and show the Homescreen.
- ➤ Perform your iPhone Settings for CarPlay
- ➤ Activate Siri.
- ➤ Update your iOS 11 to iOS 12 or 13 (see "**Update**" under Guide 1)

**Activate Siri On Your iPhone**

Homescreen: Hit on **Settings**

Settings: Hit on **Siri & Search**

Siri & Search: Put On all the activators.

**Different Ways of Connecting CarPlay from Your iPhone to Your Car**
1. Lightning to USB cable connection.
2. Bluetooth connection.
3. Wireless connection.

**Connection Process for USB Car Port**

➢ Start your Car and let the Car's Stereo boot to the Homepage.
➢ Insert the small power connector of the USB cable to your iPhone USB power port. Ensure you hear a clear click sound,
➢ Insert the second end of the USB cord into the Stereo USB port.
➢ **Once it is properly connected:** You will see the **Apple CarPlay** icon among the Apps icon on the Car's Homescreen.

**Connection Process for Car Using Wireless or Bluetooth**

➢ Press and hold down the **Voice-Command** on the Steering Wheel.
➢ **Go to Your iPhone XS or XS Max**

Homescreen: Hit on Settings.

Settings: Scroll down to hit on **General**

General: Hit on **CarPlay**

CarPlay

- ➤ Hit on **Available Car**
- ➤ Select your Car name.
- ➤ **Once it is connected:** You will see all the **Apple CarPlay** Icon among the Apps icon on the Car's Homescreen.

**On Your Touch Sensitive Stereo**

- ➤ The stereo will restart and show **Caution** information, read and hit on **I Agree**
- ➤ In few seconds the **Apple CarPLay** icon will show.
- ➤ Hit on the **Apple CarPlay.** All your iPhone Apps (e.g. Call, Music, Messages, Maps, Audiobooks, YouTube, etc.) will display on the Stereo CarPlay Screen. Press the bottom right arrow to see more Apps.

**To Add More App to the Default Apps on Your Touch Sensitive Stereo Homescreen**

Homescreen: Hit on Settings.

Settings: Scroll down to hit on **General**

General: Hit on **CarPlay**

CarPlay: Select the Name of your Car (e.g. **SUBARU**)

SUBARU: Hit on **Customize**

Customize: Scroll down the page and select from the Apps under **MORE APP** by tapping on the Add Sign in a green circle in front of the App you want to be added on the Car Stereo Homescreen.

➕ You can also add Google Map to complement Apple Map.

**To Remove Apps:** Under the **INCLUDE** list of all the default apps on the Car's Homescreen hit on Minus Sign in a red circle ⊖ at the front of the App to delete the App from the list. You can restore it by going to MORE APP and hit on Add sign.

**How You Can Rearrange The Apps On The CarPlay Homescreen**

Customize: Hit on the App and drag it either up or down within the Apps. The Apps will show on the CarPlay Homescreen exactly you arranged them on the **Customized List.**

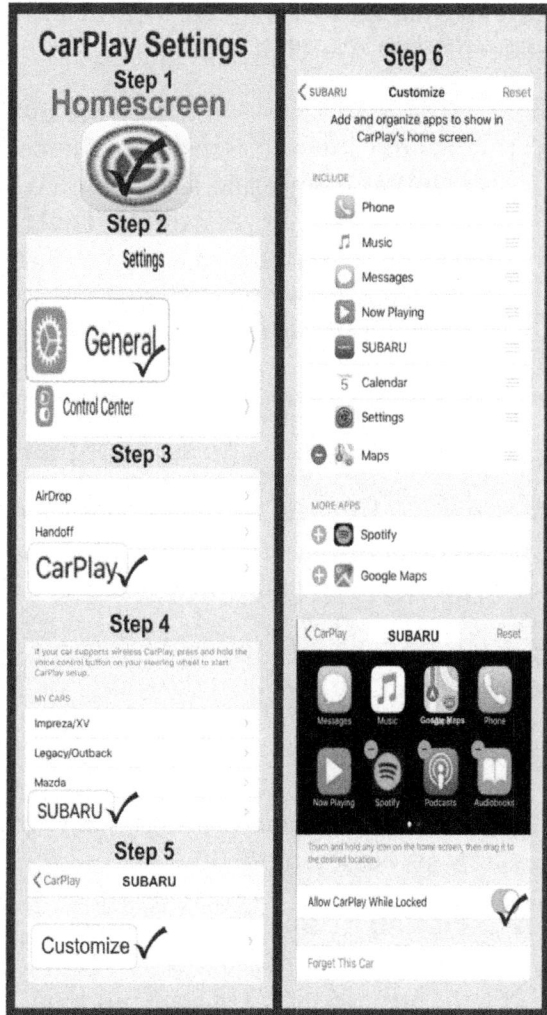

# How Siri Can Provide Solutions to CarPlay Problems

Siri is very helpful in giving reliable suggestions through the CarPlay to let you know the possible next line of actions or sending a message to someone by dictating your message directly.

You can instruct Siri to forward a call to any of your favorite contacts.

However, the type of your car will determine how you can use Siri to do what you want it to do for you.

**There three major ways you can use Siri with your CarPlay.**
1. On the Stereo Sensitive Touchscreen touch and hold **CarPlay Home** and ask Siri to do you it to do for you.
2. On the Stereo Sensitive Touchscreen touch and hold **CarPlay Dashboard** and give Siri instruction.
3. On the **Steering Wheel** press and hold the **Voice-Command button** and ask Siri what you wanted.

**To Send Message On CarPlay Through Siri**

**Homescreen:** Hit on the **Messages App** icon

**Messages:** Select the **Name of the Person** you want to send a message to. You can press on the up and down arrow to search for the recipient name up and down of the screen.

Siri icon will appear to send your message. Then dictate your message and Siri will repeat the dictated message back for confirmation.

If what you have said were correct, you can say "Perfect" and order, Siri, to "Send the message". Siri will reply to you that your message has been sent.

**How You Can Setup 3D Map Guide**

**CarPlay Homescreen:** Hit on **Map** icon

**Map:** Hit on **Destinations** at the top right of the screen

**Destination:** Select from any of these destinations:

1. **Get directions to a destination in the list:** Choose your Destination by tapping.
2. **Get direction to a nearby service:** Choose Service Category including Coffee, Gas or Parking; and choose the destination.

OR

Use Siri: Ask Siri:

> ➢ Take me to the address in the destination.
> ➢ Take me home
> ➢ Take me to the nearest fueling station or gas station
> ➢ Take me to the nearest hospital
> ➢ Take me to the nearest Shopping Mall
> ➢ Find the nearest hotel
> ➢ Tell me the location of where I am … and many others.

**How You Can Use Map on Your iPhone XS**

Homescreen: Hit on the **Maps** icon.

Maps: Hit on **Directions**

Directions: Select

> ✓ **Drive:** If you are driving
> ✓ **Walk:** If you want to trek the distance
> ✓ **Transit:** If you will be taking various transport
> ✓ **Ride:** If you want to embark on the distance with bicycle,

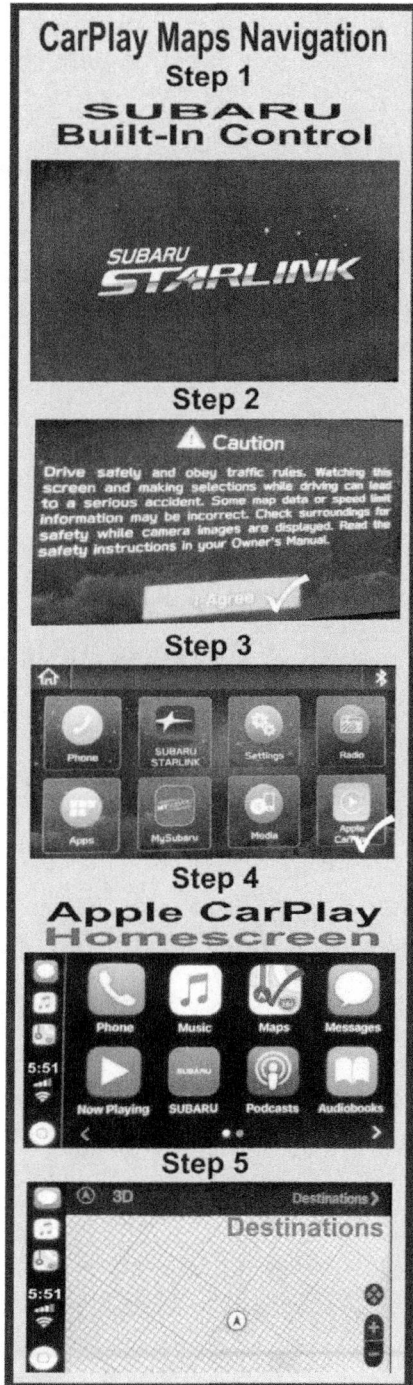

CarPlay Maps Navigation

Step 1
SUBARU Built-In Control

Step 2
⚠ Caution
Drive safely and obey traffic rules. Watching this screen and making selections while driving can lead to a serious accident. Some map data or speed limit information may be incorrect. Check surroundings for safety while camera images are displayed. Read the safety instructions in your Owner's Manual.

Step 3

Step 4
Apple CarPlay Homescreen

Step 5
Destinations

165

motorcycle, or tricycle.

> Choose the route you want. Maps will show you the shortest direction with consideration of traffic conditions.
> Hi on **Go**. For you to see the general overview of your route bearing direction.
> Hit on **Tap for Overview** in the banner. Also, you may hit on **Share ETA** to share your location with others.
> To stop the **Navigation** hit on **End** and hit on **End Route**.

**Use Siri**: Ask Siri to "**Stop Navigating**" once you have **Hands-Free Activated** (Switched "ON").

**How You Can Prevent Tolls or Highways**

**Homescreen**: Hit on **Settings**

**Settings**: Hit on **Maps**

**Maps**: Hit on **Driving & Navigation**

**Driving & Navigation**: Hit the Activator of **Tolls or Highways**

**Hint**: As soon as you start your movement, the Maps will automatically update itself to show you the most appropriate direction.

The hindrance on your route bearing could be seen on Maps iPhone by using your finger to scroll up.

Maps will protect you from missing your next turn at the beginning and the walking out of the route by showing you the perfect lane you should remain when you are driving.

# GUIDE TEN

## How You Can Accurately Track Your Health on Your iPhone XS or XS Max

This application has feature that can be used to track your daily good living and general health condition by going through the medical setting to input your health history and personal data in the Health App to see the total activities data that is generated on your iPhone and the different applications you have used so far.

Automatically Health App tracks your daily distance running exercise, gradual physical steps, walk, sleep, mental stability, fertility status, diets, weight balance... and several others. If you are also having Apple Watch it could perform the same function of tracking your daily activities and generate relative data to compare with the previous days.

More data could be gotten from all your relevant Apps such as Calendar, Reminder, Workout, Activity ... and other apps that are helping you in organizing your daily activities and execution of health projects or daily, weekly, monthly, or yearly budgets.

In some cases like a heart condition, menstrual cycle... and others, it is very important you use Apple Watch with your iPhone XS or XS Max running with iOS 13 to get a perfect prediction, benefits more from the innovativeness and efficiently loaded Health App.

However, I will discuss some of the vital activities you could track with the use of your iPhone running with iOS 12 but when it comes to the inevitable content that is only available in iOS 13 and above, I will encourage you to upgrade iOS 12 to 13 to efficiently benefit all the features on your iPhone. An example of the content is Cycle Tracking.

## *What To Do First*

You will need to provide your Medical Details in these three profile sections:

1. **Health Profile:** It contains your Name, Contact, Date of Birth, Sex, Blood Type, Fitzpatrick Skin Type, and Wheelchair.

2. **Medical ID:** It shows the same Emergency information on your iPhone or Apple watch which also contains activation of Emergency when your iPhone is Locked, Date of Birth (DOB), Medical Conditions, Medical Notes, Allergies & Reactions, Medication, Blood Type, Organ Donor, Weight, Height, and Emergency Contacts.

3. **Organ Donation:** This will enable you to register for an Organ donor through the **sign up with Donate Life.** It comprises the following data of yours; Names, DOB, Last 4 Social Security Number (SSN), Email, Address, ZIP, and Sex.

## *How You Can Set Up Your Health Profile*

Homescreen: Hit on the **Health App** icon.

Health: Hit on **Summary Tab**.

Summary: Hit on your **Profile**

168

Health App Setup
Step 1

Step 2

Step 3

Step 4

Step 5

**Picture** at the top right side of the page.

Your Name Page: Hit on **Health Profile**

**Health Profile:**

➢ Hit on **Edit** at the top right angle of the page.
➢ Provide your Age, Weight, and Height
➢ Hit on **Done** at the top right angle of the page

## *How You Can Set Up Medical ID*

Homescreen: Hit on the **Health App** icon.

Today Page: Hit on **Medical ID icon** at the right bottom of the screen ✳

Medical ID: Hit on **Create Medical ID** bar.

✳ Medical ID

➢ Hit on **Show When Locked** activation slider to enable to access Emergency when your iPhone is locked.
➢ Hit on **Add Photo** to upload your photo on the page
➢ Hit on **Add Date of Birth:** You will see the date suggested at the bottom of the screen. Scroll up until you will get to your Month/Day/Year

169

and hit on it to select.

- Hit on **Medical Condition** to type your health discomfort (e.g. Herpes, Stomach ache, Arthritis, etc.).
- Hit on **Medical Notes** to write medical history.
- Hit on **Allergies & Reactions** to write the signs and symptoms in the text field. I do not have any reaction you may write "Nil/None".
- Hit on **Medication** to write the doctor's prescription on the text field. If you do not have, you may type "Nil/None"
- Hit on **Add Blood Type** to select.
- Hit on **Organ Donor** to select "No, Yes or Not Yet"
- Hit on **Weight** to select your body weight
- Hit on **Height** to select your height.
- Hit on **Add Emergency Contact** to select your trusted loved ones' contact from your iPhone contact list.
- Hit on **Done** at the right top angle of the screen.

**To Confirm How The Emergency Settings Work**

- Press the **Power** Button to sleep and re-press the button to wake the iPhone.
- Use your Face ID to unlock the iPhone.
- Swipe up from the bottom center of the screen to see the **lock screen** with the **Emergency** at the bottom left of the screen.
- Hit on the **Emergency**
- **Emergency Call:** If you must access Medical ID, then hit the **Medical ID** at the bottom left of the screen. All the information you have provided during the setup.
- At the bottom of the Medical ID page, you will see the **Continue bar**. Hit on the **Continue** bar to complete the registration.
- Hit on **Complete Registration with Donate later** bar.
- **Thank You:** Hit on **Done** bar.

## *How You Can Setup Your Health Data*

If you have previously upgraded your iPhone XS or XS Max from iOS 12 to 13 version, the below steps will be slightly different from the advanced iOS on your iPhone XS or XS Max. However, all the steps are available in those advanced iOS.

**Homescreen:** Hit on the **Health App** icon.

**Dashboard:** You will see your **Dashboard**. There are period titles which are **Day | Week | Month | Year.** You can select any of the periods that you will be tracking your health data. To start with, select **Day** by tapping on it.

Hit on **Health Data** at the second left bottom of the screen to add different health categories such as **Body Weight, Active Calories,**

**Heart Record, Heart, Reproductive Health, Body Temperature ...** and more others.

For Instance:

- ➢ Hit on **Active Calories**
- ➢ **Active Calories:** Hit on **Add Data Point.**
- ➢ **Add Data:**
  - ✓ Type Your daily preferred Calories figure like 250
  - ✓ Hit on **Add** at the top right angle of the screen.

**Add Health Info**

You will see that the number of Calories has been increased from the recommended calories per day. But if you are not having calories on the displayed table, you could go ahead and add your daily calories.

Your iPhone will strictly use your daily recommended calories to track your daily calories used through your daily activities.

For the tracking to show on your Dashboard, then you have to activate **Show on Dashboard** slider.

Now as you are moving around, the number of your steps, distance cover in Kilometer (Km), and Calories spent (kcal) will be tracked.

**To Add More of Your Health History**

Homescreen: Hit on the **Health App** icon.

Health Data

- ➢ Hit on the **Browse** tab
- ➢ Hit on a **Category** like Activity.
- ➢ Select **Subcategory** like Steps
- ➢ Hit on **Add Data** at the top right angle of the screen.
- ➢ Type the **Date, Time,** and **Data** for the Activity.
- ➢ Hit on **Add** at the top right angle of the screen.

# How You Can Check Your Health Data

**Homescreen:** Hit on the **Health App** icon.

**Health Data:** Hit on the **Category** like **Body Measurement**

**Body Measurement:** Select your **Subcategory** like **Body Mass Index**.

**Body Mass Index**

- ➤ Put "On" the **Add to Favorite** activator.
- ➤ Hit on **Show All Data** to see all the data of the tracked activity.
- ➤ After you have confirmed what you want to know then you can back the page at the top left side of the page.

# How You Can Track All Your Favorite Categories with Your iPhone

**Homescreen:** Hit on **Health App** icon

**Today Summary:** Hit on **Summary Tab**

**Summary:** Hit on **Edit** at the top right angle of the screen page.

**Edit Favorite**

- ➤ Hit on each desirable Star to add more **Categories.** ★ .
- ➤ As soon as you have completely selected all your preferred **Favorite Categories**, the hit on **Done** at the top right side of the screen.

Hint: When you hit on each star, it will change from frame star ☆ to full blue star ★ .

# *How Organ Donation Could Be Setup on Your iPhone*

Homescreen: Hit on the **Health App** icon.

Health: Hit on **Summary Tab**.

Summary: Hit on your **Profile Picture** at the top right side of the page.

Your Name Page: Select **Organ Donor**

Organ Donor: Hit on the **Sign Up with Donate Life** bar to sign up.

Registration

- ➤ All your profile details will display, what you only need is to enter the last four-digit number of your **Social Security Number** (SSN).
- ➤ Hit on the **Continue** button below to complete your registration.
- ➤ Hit on **Complete Registration with Donate Life** at the bottom center of the screen.

**Thank You:** Hit on the **Done** button below.

Your complete registration with Donate Life will show up under your Medical ID profile as **Organ Donor-Donate Life.**

# How You Can Fix Failure of Health Tracking on Your iPhone XS or XS Max

For your health tracking steps to be functionally perfect, you need to connect your Apple Watch with your iPhone.

If you are having a challenge of not seeing your steps being tracked by Health App on your iPhone XS or XS Max then take the following steps:

Homescreen: Hit on the **Health App** icon.

Health: Hit on **Summary Tab**.

Summary: Hit on your **Profile Picture** at the top right side of the page.

Your Name Page: Under **Privacy** hit on **Devices**

Devices: Select your **Apple Watch**

Your Watch Privacy: Hit on **Privacy Settings** and activate **Fitness Tracking** by switching On the Activator.

# How You Can Make Family Sharing Working

Homescreen: Hit on the **Settings App** icon

Settings: Go to your **Profile Name** at the top

Apple ID: Select Set Up Family Sharing

Family Sharing: Hit on the "**Get Started**" button

Get Started: Select **Location Sharing** or any other feature you want to share. There might be a slightly different method of setup in various other features of family sharing available.

**Share Your Location with Your Family:** Hit on **Share Your Location** button at the bottom center of the screen. If you are not ready to share your location you can select the **Not Now** option below.

**Invite Your Family:** Hit on **Invite Family Members** bar at the bottom center.

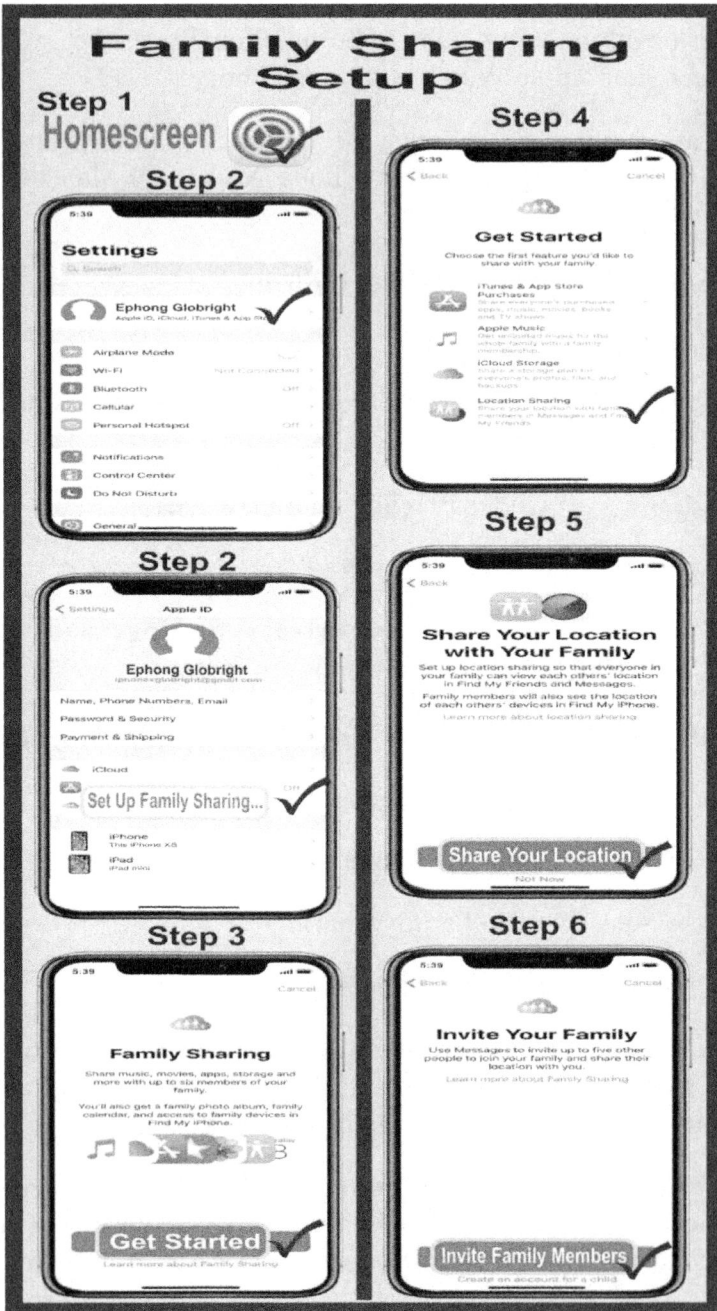

# How You Can Use Health App To Track Your Menstrual Cycle on Your iPhone

The use of Health apps to track women's menstrual cycle can only be studied and determined when you upgrade the default iOS 12 version on your iPhone to iOS 13; and watchOS 6 if you are using a watch.

However, it very important you use Apple Watch with your iPhone XS or XS Max running with iOS 13 to benefits more of the innovativeness and efficiency loaded in the Health App.

You have an opportunity of upgrading your iPhone XS or XS Max if you could follow the upgrading processing discussed in Guide One of this book.

**How You Can Set Up Every Month Menstrual Cycle on Your iPhone**

Homescreen: Hit on the **Health App** icon.

Search: Hit on the **Browse** tab at the bottom right of the screen.

Browse:

➤ Select **Cycle Tracking** among the **Health Categories**
➤ Hit on the "**Get Started**" button.

Cycle Tracking: Hit on **Options**

Options

➤ You will scroll down to select **Period Length** and swipe up to select your period duration e.g. 2 days, 3 days, 4 days, 5days, etc. The period length is the number of days you experience menstrual flow. For example, If you see the menstrual flow from Aug 2 to 5 is equal to 4days.

➤ Select **Cycle Length** and swipe up to select the appropriate days before the next menstrual cycle e.g. 25 days or 26 days etc.

Hint: If you are having some pre or post symptoms that come with your cycle you may activate all the relevant suggested contents above **Your Cycle Log.** Some of them are:

1. Spotting
2. Basal Body Temperature
3. Cervical Mucus Quality
4. Ovulation Test Result
5. Sexual Activity
6. Symptoms… and others.

**How You Can See Your Cycle Timeline**

Homescreen: Hit on the **Health App** icon.

Search: Hit on the **Browse** tab at the bottom right of the screen.

Browse: Select **Cycle Tracking** among the **Health Categories**

The Timeline will appear as:

1. **Solid Circles**: Number of days you recorded for your menstrual period.
2. **Purple Dots**: The number of days you recorded for experiencing symptoms
3. **Light Red Circle:** This is your next menstrual period Prediction.
    ✓ **For You to Hide or Display Predicted Period Days:** Select **Option** and activate the **Period Prediction** switch.

4. **Light Blue Days:** These predict your possible Fertility Window. You should not use it to guide yourself for birth control.
   ✓ **For You to Hide or Display Infertility Window:** Select **Option** and activate the **Fertility Prediction** switch.

**How You Can Know Your Possible Next Menstrual Cycle**

Homescreen: Hit on the **Health App** icon.

Search: Hit on the **Browse** tab at the bottom right of the screen.

Browse: Select **Cycle Tracking** among the **Health Categories**

Cycle Tracking

➤ Scroll down to select **Prediction** under **Cycle Log.** This will enable you to know your next menstrual cycle.
   ✓ **If you are unable to see the evaluation:** Select **Show All** before the prediction option.
➤ Scroll down to select **Statistics.** This will enable you to see all your previous menstrual period and predictive cycle length.

On Apple Watch: For You To Determine Date

➤ Launch the **Cycle Track App.**
➤ Scroll down to select **Period Prediction/Last Menstrual Period.**

**How You Can Track All Your Cycle Symptoms in Health App**

**Homescreen:** Hit on the **Health App** icon.

**Search:** Hit on the **Browse** tab at the bottom right of the screen.

**Browse:** Select **Cycle Tracking** among the **Health Categories**

**Cycle Tracking:** Hit on **Options** at front of **Cycle Log**

**Options:** Activate the **Symptoms** activator to access all the possible symptoms before/during/after the menstrual cycle. All the symptoms are listed below:

- ✓ Abdominal Cramp
- ✓ Acne
- ✓ Appetite
- ✓ Bloating
- ✓ Breast Tenderness
- ✓ Constipation
- ✓ Diarrhea
- ✓ Headache
- ✓ Hot Flashes
- ✓ Lower Back Pain
- ✓ Mood Changes
- ✓ Nausea
- ✓ Ovulation Pain
- ✓ Tiredness
- ✓ Sleep Changes

You can tap on any of the symptoms you are experiencing before or during or after the menstrual cycle to log your symptoms with Cycle Tracking.

**How You Can Record Menstrual Cycle Symptoms on Your Apple Watch.**

**On Apple Watch:**

- ➢ To launch Apple tray by pressing **Digital Crown**

- ➢ Select the **Cycle Tracking** App icon
- ➢ Hit on **Symptoms**
- ➢ Scroll through the various available symptoms and hit on various symptoms list you regularly experience before or during or after the menstrual cycle.
- ➢ Hit on **Done**

## *How You Can Set Up Prediction for Period, fertility, and Notification, through Cycle Tracking*

**Homescreen:** Hit on the **Health App** icon.

**Search:** Hit on the **Browse** tab at the bottom right of the screen.

**Browse:** Select **Cycle Tracking** among the **Health Categories**

**Cycle Tracking:** Hit on **Options**

**Options:** Hit on the activator of the below features to turn them "On".

- ➢ Activate **Period Prediction**.
- ➢ Activate the **Period Notification.**
- ➢ Activate the **Fertility Predictions**
- ➢ Activate **Fertility Notifications.**

## How You Can Record A Period Flow Level Through Cycle Tracking on Your Apple Watch

On Apple Watch

- ➢ To launch Apple tray, press **Digital Crown**

- ➢ Select the **Cycle Tracking** App icon
- ➢ In the everyday tracker above the data, Summary hit on the **Day.**
- ➢ Below Menstrual Unit hit on **Period** to record your menstrual flow. Select your period flow level by tapping on any of these options below:
  - ✓ Light
  - ✓ Medium
  - ✓ Heavy
- ➢ Hit on **Done.**

## How You Can Further Record Your Sexual Activity In Cycle Tracking

You can use this to track when last or the period you had sex with your spouse.

Option:

- ➢ Hit on **Sexual Activity**
- ➢ On the same page hit on **Sexual Activity** and select **Had Sex**.
- ➢ Select **Not Used** or **Used** to remind you of your sexual protection.

## How You Can Record Your Sexual Activity in Cycle Tracking on Your Apple Watch

On Apple Watch

- ➢ To launch Apple tray, press **Digital Crown**

- ➢ Select the **Cycle Tracking** App icon
- ➢ Hit on **Sexual Activity**
- ➢ If you had sexual intercourse, then hit on **Had Sex**

182

➤ For protection confirmation, select **Not Used** or **Used**

**How You Can Remove All Cycle Tracking in Health App On Your iPhone.**

Homescreen: Hit on the **Health App** icon.

Search: Hit on the **Browse** tab at the bottom right of the screen.

Browse: Select **Cycle Tracking** among the **Health Categories**

Cycle Tracking: Scroll down to select **View Cycle Tracking Items**

View Cycle Tracking Items: Hit on every **Category Log** you wanted to remove.

➤ Scroll down to the bottom region to hit on **Show All Data.**
➤ At the top right angle of the screen hit on **Edit.**
➤ Hit on the **Remove icon** beside the data you wanted to remove.
➤ Hit on **Delete.**
➤ Hit on **Done** at the top right angle of the screen.

# *Easy Ways of Knowing the Data Source from Several Sources*

Health App always makes use of the same data from different sources like Apple Watch, iPhone, and iPod. If you are using several Apple devices that are connected with iPhone XR, it very important as a user to specifically know which of the Apple device is responsible for the data making.

You can set your iPhone to be the major source that Health App should be used for data generation, instead of using all available Bluetooth devices. This method is called the **Prioritization of Device.**

Homescreen: Hit on the **Health App** to launch the page.

Summary: Hit on the **Browse** icon tab.

Browse: Hit on a **Category** such as **Activity**.

Activity: Select the **Subcategory** such as Steps or Walk & Running or any other one.

Hint: But if you are unable to see the subcategory you are looking for, then you can scroll up to access the Searching tool at the top of the page. Hit the field and enter the **Subcategory** and it will appear.

**Steps:** Swipe up to select **Data Sources & Access**

Hint: You will see all the Sources that are responsible for the make of the Steps' Data will be enlisted.

**How You Can Access All The General Sources For The Health App**

Homescreen: Hit on the **Health App** to launch the page.

Summary: Hit on **Profile Picture** at the top right of the page.

Your Profile Name Page: Move down of the page to Privacy and hit on **Apps or Devices.**

You will see all the Sources that enable Health App to generate those Data.

**How You Can Assign Sources for Data**

This will enable you to prioritize sources for the making of a particular subcategory data in the Health App.

Homescreen: Hit on the **Health App** to launch the page.

Summary: Hit on the **Browse** icon tab.

Browse: Hit on a **Category** such as **Activity**

Activity: Select the **Subcategory**

**Subcategory:** You will go down the page and select **Data Source & Access.**

**Data Source & Access:** Hit on **Edit**

➢ Touch and Hold down **Change Order** Button at the front of the Data Source. ▤

➢ You can either **Drag Up** or **Down** the **Data Source** on the lists.

**If you do not want a Data Source to generate Data for the Subcategory:** Deactivate the **Activation Switch**

# BONUS GUIDE

## *The Protective Accessory for iPhone XS or XS Max*

Although, Apple organization has already designed prolong durable iPhone XS or XS Max outer ringside to satisfy the user by using a stainless glass body to repel water and easy to clean when it is having a contact with hard stain or covered with dust.

But, the is not adequate for those that want the iPhone to be a fully protected incidence that may damage the sensitive screen and the backside of the iPhone.

Apple company only provided partial protection, not total protection that could prevent the iPhone XS's or XS Max's screen from damage when it suddenly falls on a hard pointed surface. As a result, it very important to provide more sustainable additional **Screen Protector and quality body Casing**.

Now the choice of providing absolute protection for your iPhone XS or XS Max is in your hand. If you are looking for where you could get quality and durable casing or screen protectors, there are many quality and smart iPhone body Case and Screen Protectors on the "Amazon Platform", that will also add beauty to your iPhone look "appearance". Search for anyone you like and make an order.

**How to Fix Screen Protector without Bubble on the Screen**

Some of the Screen protectors come with a sachet of Wet Wipe and Dry Wipe.

**Materials You Need:**

Alcohol Swap, or Isopropyl Alcohol, Microfiber Cleaning Cloth (MCC) (e.g., Magicfiber, e-cloth,), Dust Removing Sticker (DRS), Thick Paper Business Card

**First Method**

1. Switch off your iPhone
2. Use alcohol swap or add small Isopropyl alcohol into a clean cotton to clean up the surface of the iPhone screen to remove oil on the screen surface. Ensure you clean from inside to the edges of the iPhone.
3. Use the available MCC to clean the iPhone screen surface from edge to edge to completely remove dust.
4. Use a side of DRS to sweep the screen surface from the top to the bottom of the screen. Just 2 to 3 times (Optional).
5. Remove the protective paper/nylon at the front of the Screen Protector.
6. Gently hold the Screen front the left and right sides with your hand.
7. Slowly bend down the head of the Screen protector toward the head of the iPhone. Use your second hand to support the screen protector at the opposite end to align the screen protector edge with the iPhone top edge.
8. Slowly move your hand holding the screen down; with the help of the thumb of the second hand press the screen surface to remove any possible bubble and use the Thick Card to slightly press the screen down and sweep the surface toward the bottom of the iPhone side by side as you are moving down your hand to prevent bubble(s).

**Second Method**

1. Remove the protective nylon or paper on the screen protector surface.
2. Position the side of the screen protector at one side of the iPhone to ensure that the screen is at the center of the iPhone. Some screen protectors come with tape stickers but if you do not have never mind.
3. Position the upper end of the screen protector at the same upper end of your iPhone XS or XS Max and gently move down your hand until it gets to the opposite end.
4. Allow it to spread and use the Microfiber Cleaning Cloth to press the screen surface from the top of the iPhone by

moving your hand from left to right till you will get to the bottom of the iPhone to prevent bubble. **Or**

**Third Method: Nylon or Paper Sticker Support Method**

➢ If you have a paper sticker, cut three of 4cm of paper sticker each. Stick 2cm from the length of the paper sticker at the left, right, and bottom center.

➢ Gently position the screen protector top edge at the exact top edge of the iPhone screen.

➢ Look at both sides, and ensure the screen protector is aligned with the iPhone edge.

➢ Use the remaining 2cm paper sticker at the left and right to adhere to the screen protector with the main iPhone body.

➢ Hold the opposite paper sticker to slowly bring down the screen protector to the surface of the iPhone XS or XS Max.

➢ Use clean soft MCC to rub the surface of the protective screen from left to right to prevent bubbles as shown in the below pictures.

# Horizontal View

**Clean Soft Fabric Cotton**

**Paper Sticker**

**Opposite Paper Sticker**

**Folded Paper Sticker**

Use the opposite paper sticker to pull down the Screen Protector

# Vertical View

**Rub the surface with soft fabric cotton**

189

# REFERENCE

SUPPORT.APPLE.COM/EN-US

# INDEX

**A**

A12 Biotic Chip 14
Accessibility Shortcut 55
Accessory 182
Account
  Icloud account 84
  Mail or Email account 88,
  90, 108 – 114,
Activator 20, 55, 60, 65, 75,
90, 97 – 98
Activate 20,
Active 158
Active Calories 170
Adapter 15 – 16, 34,
Address
  Email Address 37, 76,
  112 – 113.
  Home Address 167
  Siri 163
  Web Address 119, 121, 137,
  Yahoo Address 110
Adobe Acrobat 17
Adjuster 67
Agree 32, 37, 46, 50
AirDrop 57 – 57, 121
AirPlay 60,
Airplane Mode 52,
Alarm 24, 54, 56, 64 – 65. 115
Album 59, 131, 141,
Alert 64
*Alphanumeric Code 83
Allergies 167, 169
Ambient 13
Andriod 9, 23, 33, 34, 36,
41 – 42, 46 – 51, 53, 103
Animoji 21, 27, 103 – 106.
Advance 119
  Advanced Bokeh 12
  Advanced Contrast 12
  Advanced Features 22, 142

Advanced iPhone 29
Advanced Calculator 54
AE (Autoexposure)/AF(Autofocus)
Lock 129, 130
API
  Fetch API Request 123
  Visual Viewport API 124
Applications (Apps) 21 – 28, 30, 36,
  39, 40, 42, 45, 47 – 49, 51, 52, 55,
  60, 62, 67 – 69, 71, 72, 73, 76, 84
  – 86, 89, 95, 105, 117, 121, 125,
  155, 160 – 162, 166, 176
  Apps' Icon 71
  Apps' Pages 72
Apple
  Apple Analytics, 38, 46,
  Apple Book 81,
  Apple CarPlay 159 – 165,
  Apple Devices 76, 121, 154,
  Apple Earpods 116
  Apple ID, 31, 36, 37,
  39, 40, 43, 76 – 81,
  84, 85, 100, 152,
  Apple iPhone 76
  Apple Macintosh Computer
  (Mac) 29
  Apple Map 161
  Apple Music 59
  Apple Password 37
  Apple Pay 38, 46,
  46, 76, 81, 119
  Apple Store 60, 81
  Apple TV Remote 55
  Apple Wallet 46
  Apple Watch 23, 166,
  167, 174, 176, 178 – 181
  Apple's Image 47
Audio 13, 58
  Audio Call 27, 86, 100 – 102,
  Audio Card 60

Audio Music 28, 34, 41, 105
Audio Playback 12
Audio Sound 54, 60
Audio Voice 104, 107 – 108.
Audio Zoom 12
Audiobooks 59, 161
Auto
    Autofill 118
    Auto-Capitalization 111
    Auto-Correction 111
    Auto HDR 138
    Auto-Lock 74 – 75, 155
    Auto-Reply 66
    Auto-Sleep 66
    Auto-Switch Off 71
Automatic 141 (Timer 24)
    (Apps 22, 69)
    Automatic Setup 21, 33,
    43, 51, 108, 110, 116
    Automatic Transfer 39, 42
    Automatic Update 62, 84,
    Automatic Favorite Call 65
    (Web 121)
    Anti-Shake 148
    Find My 152
    iCloud 153
    Health App 166
    Map 165
    Message App 104
    Photo Library 125
    Safari App 117, 119

**B**

Battery 10 – 11, 21 – 22,
23, 25, 28, 34, 42, 47
Background 12, 127, 132,
Back Camera 11, 20, 126, 137,
Backup 14, 29, 31, 36
42-43, 84-85, 90, 158
Badge 61
Balance 145
    White Balance 143, 146-147

Weight Balance 166
Banner 61, 165,
Basic 52, 64
Beginner 9, 33, 47,
Blank anchor target 123
Block Pop-up 118
Block All Cookies 119
Block top-level redirects by third 124
Bluetooth 17, 33, 39-41,
47, 52-53, 57, 66, 160
Bokeh 12
Bold Text 19, 75
Bookmark 117
Bonus Guide 34, 183
Brightness 54, 57, 73-74, 129, 142,
Burst 133, 143
Button 16, 27, 40, 41, 43, 103, 104,
    117, 120, 163, 173, 174-176
    Activation Button 43, 55, 65,
    73, 111, 116, 119, 123-124
    Call Button 92, 95, 97, 101, 103
    Cancel/Delete Button 94, 105, 107
    End Button 92, 101-102
    Power/Switch Button 16, 18,
    20, 24, 34, 43, 48, 61-63,
    65-66, 75, 116, 169,
    Recording Button 134-135
    Send Button 104-107
    Silence Button 16, 64
    Siri Button 17, 116, 140
    Volume Button 16, 24, 61
Bubbles 69, 107, 183
Browser 21, 23,

**C**

Cable 15-16, 31, 34, 53, 160
Calculator 26, 52, 54-55
Calendar 25, 59, 78, 84, 95
Calls 62-65, 77, 86-88, 92-98
100-103, 106, 115-116, 161, 169
Calories 28, 170-171

Camera 11-13, 22-27, 35, 39, 44-45, 52, 81-82, 105, 119, 125-151,

Capacity 10, 12, 14-15, 71,

Card 17

    Apple Pay Credit Card 76, 85,

    Audio Card 60,

    CardDAV 91

    SIM Card 15, 18-19, 34, 42, 89-90

CarPlay 159-165

Catalina 29

Case 34, 183

Cellular 17, 23, 25, 28, 31, 39-41, 52, 62, 86, 117, 141, 153

Certification 17

Chat 27, 71,102-107

Code 78, 83, 137-138

Color 19, 106, 127, 130-131, 138-139, 146-147

Components 9-18

Computer 29, 34, 41-42, 157

Conference Audio/Video 86, 100, 102

Contacts 27, 59, 65, 78, 84, 87-99

Control 20, 25, 31, 33, 39-40, 52-57 57, 60, 66, 73-74, 112, 115, 129, 137, 141-142, 144-146, 178

Cool 42, 121, 130, 146-147

Copy 108,

Create 76,

    Album 140

    Apple ID 76,

    Customized Control 56,

    Face ID 81

    Files 68

    Medical ID 168

    New Contact 93

    Passcode 36, 49, 78, 82-83,

Custom 96

    Custom Alphanumeric Code 83

    Custom Number Code 83

Customize 70, 73, 161-162

    Customized Controls 9, 52, 73,

    Customized Animoji 27, 52, 106

Cycle (check Menstrual Cycle) 166, 176

**D**

Dashboard 163, 170-171

Data 39-42, 45-50, 53, 60, 82, 100, 117, 141, 155, 158, 166, 170-172, 181

Deactivate 20, 53,

Default 52-55, 69, 83, 87, 95, 98, 99, 113, 148, 150, 161-162, 176

Desktop 118

Devices 29, 46, 53, 76, 84, 121, 150, 153-154, 157, 174, 182,

Dialog Box 40, 49, 60, 67-70, 88 -90,120, 155, 159

Dictation Messages 107-108, 111, 115

Digital

    Crown 180-181

    Single-Len Reflex Camera 146

Donation 167, 173

Drive 33, 85, 113, 117, 164.

Dual Camera 127 or SIM 18, 98

**E**

Ejector (SIM) 15

Emergency 62-63, 65, 167-169

Email 37, 76-81, 87-99, 93, 100, 102, 108-110, 112-113, 154, 167

Emoji 104

End Call 92

Experimental 123

Exposure (Camera) 129, 142

Express Settings 37 (Card 17)

External Buttons 16, 64

**F**

Face ID 25-26, 35-36, 44-45, 49, 59, 66, 81-84, 155, 169

FaceTime 27, 86, 100-103, 106,

Family 98, Sharing 152, 157, 174

Favorites 65, 87, 98, 115, 118

Fetch API Request 123
File 67-68, 118, 130, 141, 150-151
Filter 12, 125, 130-131,
Find My 26, 39, 79, 85, 152, 157, 159
Finder 30-31, 155
Flash 13, 23, 52, 54, 90, 125, 132, 179
Focus 11, 35, 44, 81, 127-129, 137, 143
Format 17, 24, 54, 108, 117, 134, 141, 143, 150-151
Freezing iPhone 61
Front-Facing Camera 13, 20, 35, 44, 81

**G**
Gigabyte 14
Gmail 90, 108
Google 47, 108 115, 118, 153, 155, 161,
Greeting 95
Grids 143, 145

**H**
HDR (High Dynamic Range) 11, 138
Health App 21, 25, 84, 166-184
Hepatic Ring 98
Highways 165
Highest Efficiency 133
Histogram 147-148,
History 94, 119, 166, 169, 171,
Home Screen 22, 25-28, 67-77
Hotspot 40, 47, 53
HTM/HTML 18

**I**
IP68 Certification 17
iCloud 14, 24, 26, 29, 36, 42-43, 59, 77
-78, 84, 108, 113, 117, 119, 139-141, 150-151, 153-155, 158
Icons 22-23, 52, 67, 71, 119, 143, 154
Identity (ID) 25, 76-85.
Image 11, 22, 31, 44, 50, 65-71, 104, 119, 125-136, 144-149.
IMAP 110
Infrared Sensor 13

iOS 21, 26, 29-32, 82, 159, 170, 176
    iPhone XS and XS Max Applications (App) 21-28
    Basic Features 64
    Body Parts Details 9-18
    Camera & Photo 125
    CarPlay Connection 159
    Charging Method 15
    Control Center 52
    Create Security IDs 76
    Health Tracking 166
    iOS Upgrading 21
    Lost iPhone 152
    Protective Accessories 185
    SIM Insertion 18
    Setup 33
    Video & Music 57
ISO 146
iTunes 26, 30, 58-60, 81, 86

**J**
JavaScript 123
JPEG 17, 113, 143, 150-151
Junks 97

**K**
Kelvin 146
Keyboard 25, 37, 41, 48, 83, 102, 104
106-107, 111-112, 120, 135
Keychain 85
Keynote 17, 26, 60, 113
Keypad 11, 36, 50, 92-97

**L**
Light Blue Days 178
Lighting Effects 12, 15, 127
Lightning to USB Cable 13, 29, 31, 160
LTE 23
Live Chat 102-105
Live Photo 27, 100, 125, 132,
Live Wallpaper 69-70
Lock Screen 22-25, 56, 64, 66, 69, 116

Low Data Mode 62, 73-74
Low Power Mode 73-74
**M**
Macintosh Computer (Mac) 29-31
   MacOS Catalina 29-31
   MacOS Mojave 29
Malfunction of iPhone 61, 71
Magnification (Camera Zoom) 12,
126-127
Mail App 28, 86-93, 98, 108-114
Map App 26, 153-158, 161, 163-165
Manual Setup 33-39, 47, 109, 116
Manual Update 37, 46,
Meaning of Terms 20
Media Capabilities 124
Medical ID 167-167
Memoji 27, 103, 106
Menstrual Cycle 28, 176-180
Message App 103-108
Microphone 13, 107, 119
Microsoft 17
Minimized App 72, 114
Mobile Data 122
Modes 125-127, 134
Music App 26, 28, 34, 41, 57-58
   Music Panel 52-53
**N**
Network 23, 29-31, 33-35, 39-42,
47-48, 52-53, 85, 112, 117, 119,
122-123, 141, 153
Night Shift 11, 58, 54, 74
Notifications 23-24, 61-62, 64-65,
98-99,
138, 158-159, 180
Numeric Code 83

**O**
Old iPhone 39-47,
OLED (Organic Light Emitting
Diode) 11-12
Open Pages 71-72, 121
Outcoming Mail 110

**P**
Pano Mode 125-126, 150
Passcode 26, 31, 36, 39, 44, 49, 61,
78, 81, 82-84,
Password 29, 35, 37, 40, 48, 59,
77-81, 84-85, 90-91, 95-95, 109,
153-154,
Personal Computer (PC) 29-31, 34,
36, 41-42, 46, 53, 58-59, 90, 141,
153, 155
Personal Hotspot 40, 53,
Photo App 59, 100, 113, 125-141,
168
Pictures 24, 27, 55, 58, 108, 114,
125, 131, 133, 138-140, 143,
Playlist 59,
Power Button 15-16, 18, 34, 48,
61, 63, 66, 169
Power Port 15, 33, 160
Precautions 71,
Prediction 166, 177-178, 180
Predictive 111, 185
Prevent 64, 79, 81, 95,119, 122-
123, 139, 148, 165, 185-187
Problems 19, 163-165,
ProCamera (Professional Camera)
141-151
Profile 22, 43, 76, 79-80, 84, 152,
167-168, 173-174, 183
Portrait 12, 53, 81, 127, 131, 135
**Q**
Quick Response (QR) Code 138
**R**
Rearrange Apps 67-69, 162
Reactivate 122
Recent Contacts 39, 93-94,
   Download 118
   Photo 135
   Video 105
Record Video/Slo-mo 133
Recording Button 104-108
Recover Forgot Apple ID 80,
Reminder 17, 28, 78, 94, 111, 166

Remove Animoji/Memoji 103
  Contacts 88
  Grid 136 (Page 72)
Reply Text Messages 103-104
Rescue Yourself 62
Reset Voicemail 96
Ring
Ringtone/Ring 65, 93, 98-99
S
Safari 26, 78, 86, 114, 117-124
Scan 137
Schedule Time 65
Screen 33-39, 52, 57, 107, 129,
136, 185-187
    Display 11-12, 130-151
    Home Screen 22, 25-28, 52-
56
    67, 69, 71,
    Lock Screen 22-25, 52-55, 56
    Protector 185-187
Searching Tool 20, 24, 60, 95,
116, 118, 140
Security ID 25, 66, 76-85, 119,
173
Settings App 26,
Setup 33, 43, 96, 100, 109-110,
159, 163,
167, 170, 173, 176, 180
Sexual Activity 177, 181
Share Icon 117, 121, 135, 165
Location 153, 158, 174
Sign In 59, 76, 79-80, 84, 110,
152
Silence Mode 18, 64, 98,
SIM 18-19, 23, 42, 52, 89-90, 98
Siri 26, 86, 115-117, 118, 140,
160, 162-164
Sleep Action 66
Slo-mo 135
SOS 63
Sound 53, 60, 64, 98-99, 107,
154-155
Speaker 13, 60, 94,

Span 15,
Stereo 159-163
Swiping Method 72
Syncing 58
T
Telephoto 126-128
Text Message 101, 103-104, 106-108
Timeline 177
Timer 38, 52, 54, 125, 131
Track Health 166, 172, 174, 176,
179, 181,
Transfer Data 39, 42, 47
U
Unbreakable Passcode 82
Unwanted Callers 97-98
Update 29-32, 37, 46, 159, 165
Upgrade 21, 29-32, 37, 166, 170, 176
USB 15-16, 29, 31, 54, 40, 160
V
Vibration 64, 98
Video 13-14, 20, 22, 27, 34, 41, 57-
60, 100-103, 105, 113, 125-126, 133-
135, 139-141
View Controls 25, 56
Viewfinder 44-45, 125-130, 136,
139, 142
Voice-Command 160
Voice Dictation 115
Voice Message 107
Voicemail 95-98
Volume 16, 20, 24, 52-54, 61, 63
W
Wake Action 66
Wallpaper 69-70
Webpage 117, 120-123
Wi-Fi Network 17, 23, 24-42, 47-49,
52-53,
112, 122-123, 141, 153
Wireless 17, 160-161
Write Message 112
Z
Zoom 12, 39, 119, 125-127
ZIP 17